HERALDIC
DESIGNS AND ENGRAVINGS

A HANDBOOK AND DICTIONARY
OF
HERALDIC TERMS

REVISED AND ENLARGED 1966 EDITION

Illustrations and Engravings by
J. M. BERGLING

Heraldic Terms and Technical Work by
A. TUSTON HAY

Edited and Published by
V. C. BERGLING

Coral Gables, Florida 33134 U.S.A.

Printed by
EXCELLA PRES
Chicago, U.S.A.

Technical Art Books   *By* J. M. BERGLING

- Art Alphabets and Lettering

- Art Monograms and Lettering - *Complete Deluxe Volume - or*
  Condensed Edition

- Ornamental Designs and Illustrations

- Heraldic Designs and Engravings Illustrated Manual
  Technical Manual by A. Tuston Hay

- General Style Charts for Design Selection

HERALDIC SERVICES: *References and Search obtainable on Family Coats of Arms, Paintings and Engravings, Rare Books.*

✤

For information write the Publisher.

✤

IN preparing this work, we have attempted to present Heraldry to the beginner in as interesting and concise a form as possible. We have assembled over 2000 illustrations of armorial bearings and figures used in the Science of Heraldry. To this, we have added a dictionary of Heraldic terms. We believe, from bitter examples, that a knowledge of Heraldry can not be obtained by looking up terms in a dictionary. For this reason, we have made several departures from the works extant.

First, we have arranged the figures and terms so that many cross references are necessary. This was done so that many similar figures and some duplicates could be placed together where the differences would be seen by comparison. The student of Heraldry often has a figure or position in mind or in hand, but has no idea of its correct Heraldic term, and could not, therefore, use the average Heraldic dictionary to advantage. With this handbook, it is possible to find the similar figure, and from that get the correct term.

The second departure is that definitions are made as simple as is compatible with thoroughness. The English words for colours and metals are used, and there are no abbreviations.

Many Heraldic terms have several synonyms and various spellings. We use the various synonyms and forms of spelling throughout the work in order to acquaint the student with them.

We are, of course, extremely interested in Heraldry, its history, and the thousands of interesting anecdotes and tales connected with the lore of the times. Our big trouble has been to avoid wandering off as new subjects bring to mind an interesting yarn, and that one, another, *ad infinitum*. We do believe that in order to obtain even a nodding acquaintance with the subject, one should carefully read *all* of the text.

Foreword

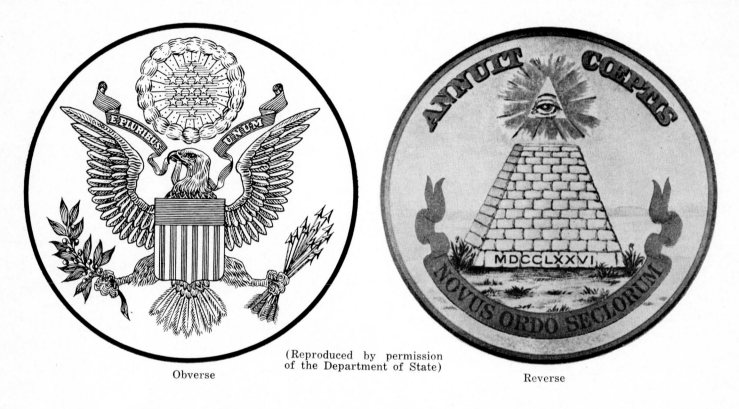

Obverse

Reverse

The Seal of the United States

ARMS. Paleways of thirteen pieces, argent and gules; a chief, azure; the escutcheon on the breast of the American eagle displayed proper, holding in his dexter talon an olive branch, and in his sinister a bundle of thirteen arrows, all proper, and in his beak a scroll, inscribed with the motto, "E Pluribus Unum."

For the CREST. Over the head of the eagle, which appears above the escutcheon, a glory, or, breaking through a cloud, proper, and surrounding thirteen stars, forming a constellation, argent, on an azure field.

REVERSE. A pyramid unfinished. In the zenith, an eye in a triangle, surrounded with a glory proper. Over the eye these words, "Annuit Coeptis." On the base of the pyramid the numerical letters MDCCLXXVI, and underneath the following motto, "Novus Ordo Seclorum."

Foreword to the 1966 Revised Edition

IN the fifteen years that have elapsed since our last edition, there has been little change in Heraldry. Because of its antiquity, fifteen years is a mere dot in time. This period has, however, seen in America a very marked and quite gratifying growth of interest in things Heraldic. We like to think that in some small way we have been responsible for this increased interest. Armorial Bearings are extremely attractive decorations, and if properly executed and placed, are in excellent taste. They give a certain personalization to a dwelling — a warmth — a pride of family — a closer connection with one's ancestors.

There are now many companies entirely devoted to the crafting of Heraldic Devices, in a wide variety from tietacs and door knockers, to huge beautifully executed wall plaques, and sumptuous rugs of British wool. The prices range from a few dollars to thousands, and the degree of correctness is almost as wide as the price range, although not necessarily in direct ratio.

In the matter of items personal, people of Scottish ancestory are even more fortunate, in that most of them have an ancestor of the same surname who belonged to a Clan or Sept of a Clan. This opens a whole new group of things out of the past with which they can identify themselves.

In ancient Scotland the Celts developed the Clan, or family system, to a very high degree, and the Chief was virtually a King, and was given amazing allegiance by his relatives. In many cases, relatives by marriage with a different surname, formed branches, or "Septs," and though the surname was different, each member of these Septs was as much a part of the Clan as anyone. Each Clan had its own pattern of cloth that belonged to that Clan alone. Many of the larger Clans had separate branches, and sometimes Septs, that had their own tartan, usually slightly differenced from that of the main or original line. These various Setts (patterns), although each different for each Clan, were similar in their design. Many people erroneously refer to these patterns as plaids. They are not plaids. A Plaid is a garment; the pattern is a Tartan. Many Scottish Clans have a "Hunting Tartan," more subdued to blend with the forest, than the colorful "Dress or Battle Tartan." Some of the large Clans have a special Tartan for the Chief and his immediate family.

Probably the Tartans most widely used in America are the "Royal Stewart" red sett and the "Royal Stewart Dress." Many Scottish Tartans are used in commercial packaging, such as "McGregor" for McGregor Sportswear, "Bruce" for Bruce Floor Polish, "Wallace" for Scotch Brand Tapes, and in Miami, Florida, the tops of the trucks of the Mary MacIntosh Laundry Service are painted to resemble the Tartan of Clan Chattan, of which the McIntoshes are hereditary chiefs. Also quite popular in America is the "Black Watch" Tartan. This Tartan belongs to the famous 42nd Royal Highland Regiment.

For people of Scottish ancestry who cannot properly identify themselves with any Clan or Sept of a Clan, there are several "district" Tartans, and Caledonia Tartan, Jacobite Tartan which they may call their own. The Clergy has a Tartan. There is a "Royal Stewart Bonnie Prince Charlie" Tartan that was differenced for the glamorous, though ill-starred Prince, who last carried the Stewart Banner in rebellion against George III.

Another family item, for those who can establish con-nection with the Clan, is the Clan Badge. The Clan Badge is made up of the Crest (see page 13 — II) of the Chief of the Clan, encircled by a belt, and the whole backed by the Clan Tartan.

Most Clans have a "Plant" Badge. Originally, a piece of the living plant was cut off and pinned to the cap, in place of and sometimes with, the above mentioned badge. Some Clans have two or more plant Badges — e.g., Clan Campbell — Wild Myrtle and Fir Club Moss; Clan Gordon — Ivy; Clan MacLeod — Red Whortleberry.

Most Clans have their own War Cry, frequently taken from some spot in their district — e.g., Clan Buchanan — "Clar Innis" (an island in Loch Lomond); Clan MacArthur — "Eisd! O Eisd!" ("Listen! O Listen!"); Clan Mac-Dougall — "Buaidh no bas" ("Victory or Death"). For those clans which had adopted no War Cry, the Clan name was repeated — e.g., "A Douglas! A Douglas!" — "A Gordon! A Gordon!", followed by "Rally Round Me!"

Many Clans have their own Pipe Music, and it is said "if there's a wee drap o' heather in ye, ye're a child of the mist, and the wild skirlin' o' the pipes will grip the marrow o' your bones."

Scottish Tartans, Garments, Badges, War Cries, Pipe Music, etc. are studies in themselves, and many very interesting and authoritative books are available on the subjects. Our limited scope allows us to touch only the high spots, as it were. A letter to the author, in care of the publisher, will bring an attempt to answer any question about sources.

A. Tuston Hay

The President's Seal

Executive Order No. 10860
Coat of Arms, Seal and Flag
of the President of the United States

(Reproduced by permission
of Special Counsel to the President)

By virtue of the authority vested in me as President of the United States, it is hereby ordered as follows:

SECTION I.   The Coat of Arms of the President of the United States shall be of the following design:

SHIELD: Paleways of thirteen pieces argent and gules, a chief azure; upon the breast of an American eagle displayed holding in his dexter talon an olive branch and in his sinister a bundle of thirteen arrows all proper, and in his beak a white scroll inscribed "E PLURIBUS UNUM" sable.

CREST: Behind and above the eagle a radiating glory or, on which appears an arc of thirteen cloud puffs proper, and a constellation of thirteen mullets argent.

The whole surrounded by white stars arranged in the form of an annulet with one point of each star outward on the imaginary radiating center lines, the number of stars conforming to the number of stars in the union of the Flag of the United States as established by chapter 1 of title 4 of the United States Code.

SEC. 2.   The Seal of the President of the United States shall consist of the Coat of Arms encircled by the words "Seal of the President of the United States."

SEC. 3.   The Color and Flag of the President of the United States shall consist of a dark blue rectangular background of sizes and proportions to conform to military and naval custom, on which shall appear the Coat of Arms of the President in proper colors.   The proportions of the elements of the Coat of Arms shall be in direct relation to the hoist, and the fly shall vary according to the customs of the military and naval services.

SEC. 4.   The Coat of Arms, Seal, and Color and Flag shall be as described herein and as set forth in the illustrations and specifications which accompany this order and which are hereby made a part thereof.   These designs shall be used to represent the President of the United States exclusively.

SEC. 5.   This order shall become effective on July 4, 1960, and Executive Order No. 10823 of May 26, 1959, shall be superseded as of that date.

DWIGHT D. EISENHOWER

THE WHITE HOUSE
February 5, 1960.

U.S. Army Photograph

Above is a reproduction of the distinguishing flag designed for, and presented to General Omar N. Bradley, as Chairman, Joint Chiefs of Staff. Designed by the Heraldic Branch of the Army and quoted in part from their description, the flag is made up as follows:

The colors, divided diagonally from the upper corner on the pike to the lower corner of the fly, are medium blue above and white below. The central design consists of an American Eagle with its wings outspread in horizontal position. On its chest is a shield with blue chief representing Congress joining the colonies into unity, and a paly of 13, seven white and six red representing the thirteen original colonies. The eagle, which faces the pike, the point of honor, is holding three gold arrows in its talons representing the Army, the Navy and the Air Force. The position of the Chairman of the Joint Chiefs of Staff is indicated by four stars, each with one point upward, placed on a diagonal line, two to each side of the eagle. Stars on the blue field are white and those on the white are blue. This flag will be used by the Chairman on ceremonial occasions. A similar flag will be used in the field, small boat and automobile flags will be displayed, and plates bearing this insignia will be attached to vehicles, aircraft and small boats when used by the Chairman of the Joint Chiefs of Staff.

Coat Arms == of 3d Infantry

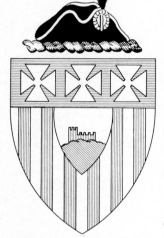

(Repro. permission of Department of the Army, Institute of Heraldry, U.S.A.)

BLAZON

SHIELD: Paly of thirteen argent and gules on a chief azure three crosses patée of the first, an inescutcheon of the like with a mount vert issuing from base and crowned with battlements of the second.

CREST: On a wreath argent and azure an infantry officer's cocked hat sable trimmed white (1784 pattern) with a cockade of the third centered of the fourth and plumed sable.

MOTTO: Noli me tangere.

When desired, the shield of the coat of arms may be encircled with an infantry officer's dress belt (paragraph 2, Special Regulation 42, 1917) or bar tierced celestial blue edged sable inscribed with the motto lettered of the like, with the buckle plate of the period of the first at top; the arms and belt surmounting a triangular bayonet of the Civil War era and the Regiment's drum major's Chapultepec Baton in saltire all proper, the baton being the one made from the City of Mexico flag pole at the time of its capture, and still in the possession of the 3d Infantry.

SYMBOLISM

Having a continuous history and descent from the old First American Regiment organized under the authority of a "Resolve" of the Continental Congress of 1784, the 3d Infantry is accorded the singular honor of the shield of the Coat of Arms of the United States as the basis for its Arms. The thirteen stripes, in this instance, commemorate the conspicuous combat service of the 3d Infantry in the campaigns of Resaca de la Palma, Monterey, Cerro Gordo, Churabusco, Chapuletepec, Bull Run, Penninsula, Manassas, Fredericksburg, Chancellorsville, Gettysburg, Santiago and Luzon; the alternating colors of silver and red symbolize a constancy of honor and courage.

The chief, blue for valor and loyalty, memoralizes the Regiment's outstanding record during the Civil War; the cross patée, the badge of Sykes' Division in which the 3d served, in triple form alludes to the Regiment's numerical designation. For its participation in the battle of Bull Run, General McDowell credited the 3d Regiment, "by its gallant conduct, unflinching steadiness, and perfect order in covering the flight of the panic-striken army, saved the Union."

The inescutcheon, in the national color of Mexico, is an augmentation which honors the 3d Infantry's distinguished service during the Mexican War. At Cerro Gordo, Churusbusco and Chapultepec the Regiment marked itself with gallant assaults which carried strong defenses. Because of its vital part in the campaign resulting in the capture of Mexico City the 3d Infantry was given the honor of marching at the head of the column when the victorious Army made its triumphant entry into the city. As the 3d approached, General Winfield Scott removed his hat and turning to his staff said, "Gentlemen, take off your hats to the Old Guard of the Army."

The cocked hat of the crest commemorates the founding of the First American Regiment in 1784.

The baton is the Chapultepec Baton, made from the wood of the flag pole which in 1847 stood in front of the cathedral in the Grand Plaza in Mexico City. The head and ferrule are made from native Mexican silver. The baton, still in the possession of the 3d Infantry, was presented to the Regiment in 1848 by its Division Commander, Brigadier General Persifer F. Smith, in tribute to the part which it took in the capture of the city, and especially the heroic assault with the bayonet which it made upon the fortress of Chapultepec.

The bayonet represents the Regiment's outstanding service during the Civil War, and also its tradition to "pass in review" with bayonets fixed in commemoration of the gallant charge which took the heights of Cerro Gordo.

The officer's dress belt symbolizes the 3d Infantry's additional role as the honor and ceremonial unit, and official guard for the Nation's Capitol.

G. H. Lancaster, Engraver, Birmingham.

TO THEIR ROYAL HIGHNESSES THE Duke & Duchess of York. A Wedding Gift FROM THE ANCIENT & LOYAL PEOPLE OF WALES July 6th 1893.

Shakespeare's House, Stratford-on-Avon.

Warwick Castle.

(by permission in 1950 from The
Private Secretary to H. M. Queen Mary)

The above is reproduced from a proof of a hand-engraved plate designed by Mr. G. H. Lancaster, whose name appears at the top. This proof and also that of the Marshalled Arms of H. M. King George V and Queen Mary, as the Duke and Duchess of York, were received many years ago from Mr. Lancaster by J. M. Bergling, the original author of this book. This excellent contribution in the field of Heraldic Art and Engraving is indeed appreciated.

(Reproduced by permission of
The Under Secretary of State, London,
and Courtesy of Garter King of Arms
College of Arms, London)

The Royal Arms

Description: The Shield is of four quarters — 1st for England: Gules 3 Lions passant gardant in pale Or; 2nd, for Scotland: Or a Lion rampant within a double tressure flory counter flory gules: 3rd, for Ireland: Azure a Harp Or stringed Argent; the whole encircled with the Garter.

Above the shield is the Royal Helmet surmounted by the Crest of England; the Crown proper thereon a Lion statant gardant Or royally crowned also proper.

The dexter Supporter, for England, is a Lion gardant Or crowned as the Crest, the sinister Supporter, for Scotland, is a Unicorn Argent armed, crined and unguled Or and gorged with a coronet composed of crosses patée and fleurs de lis, a chain affixed thereto passing between the forelegs and reflexed over the back of the last. The motto is DIEU ET MON DROIT.

The compartment or decorative addition to the Arms on which the Supporters stand shows the Royal Badges of the Rose, Thistle and Shamrock.

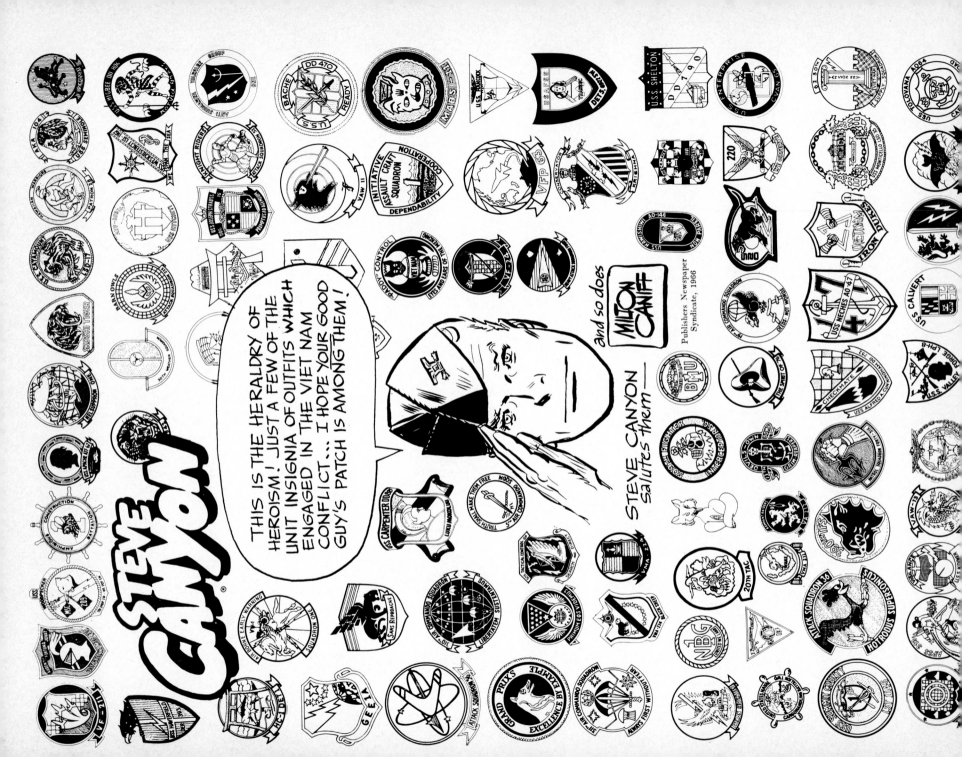

Heraldry and its Origin

This Handbook of Heraldry was compiled in the hope that it may stimulate interest in one of the truly romantic sciences of antiquity. It may also assist those who, in many branches of art, ornamental manufacture, and design, have frequent occasion to use Heraldic Devices in their work. To this end, we have attempted to show many Heraldic figures, describe them in Heraldic terms, and follow with translations into modern English.

There has been a constant increase in the general interest in Coats of Arms, Shields, Crests, etc. This interest is most gratifying to the student of Heraldry, but the abuse of terms that accompanies uninformed interest is most distasteful.

First, let us find out just what HERALDRY is: HERALDRY, as defined by Sir Francis J. Grant, Albany Herald, is "The science which teaches us how to blazon or describe in proper terms armorial bearings and their accessories." In the light of that definition, there were Heralds long before Heraldry. The office of the Herald is one of great antiquity. It is mentioned by Homer in the "Siege of Troy," and in Scripture History in Daniel, chapter iii. Many historians derive the title of Herald from Here and Hault, the champions of an army, whose duty it was to proclaim the challenges in the field of battle. It is evident that the office, from the earliest periods of history, has always been basically the same. In ancient times, it was the duty of the Herald to proclaim the will of the Monarch of the Chief Commander, to conduct negotiations between hostile or foreign powers, to regulate all state ceremonies, and in the Age of Chivalry, arrange and preside over Tournaments.

During the middle ages many of the Nobles had their own Heralds who attended them on all important occasions. There is a very popular misconception that a Herald sounded a trumpet. This delusion probably arose from the fact that the Herald was accompanied by a Royal Trumpeter. The appointment of Heralds, whose duty it was to regulate the use of armorial bearings, dates back to the latter part of the Fourteenth Century. In Scotland, the office of the Lyon King of Arms was created about 1318. In 1406, Charles VI of France formed a corporation of Heralds under Mountjoy King of Arms. In 1420, King Henry V of England created the office of Garter King of Arms, whose duty it was to control matters armorial for the Knights of the Garter. William Bruges, here shown, was the first Garter King of Arms. In 1483, King Richard III granted a charter to "The Corporation of Kings, Heralds, and Pursuivants of Arms," known as "The Heralds' College" or "The College of Arms."

The office of Earl Marshall who presides over this College has been hereditary to the Dukes of Norfolk for several hundred years. Immediately under the Earl Marshall is the Garter King of Arms. Under the Garter King are two Provincial Kings: Norroy King with jurisdiction north of the River Trent, and Clarenceux King with jurisdiction south of the River Trent. Under them are six Heralds: Chester, Windsor, Lancaster, York, Richmond, and Somerset. Under these Heralds are four pursuivants: Rouge Croix (Red Cross), Blue Mantle, Rouge Dragon, and Portcullis.

In Scotland the Lyon King of Arms was created about 1318. Under this rank were the Heralds: Rothesay, Marchmont, Snowdoun, Albany, Ross, Islay, Ireland, and Orkney. Under these Heralds were the pursuivants: Carrick, Unicorn, Aliszai, Dragance, Diligence, Dingwall, Montrose, Bute, Ormond, Falkland, Kintyre, March, and Ettrick. In 1867 the number of Heralds and pursuivants under the Lyon King were limited to three of each, to be reduced as vacancies occurred. The three Heralds are now Marchmont, Rothesay, and Albany. The three pursuivants are now Unicorn, Dingwall, and Carrick.

Since 1943 there is no longer an Ulster King of Arms for Ireland. All functions which were previously performed by Ulster King of Arms are now formally invested in the Chief Herald of Ireland whose office is at Dublin Castle. He is concerned solely with what we call the Irish Free State or Eire. The six north-eastern counties of Ireland called Ulster, now come for heraldic jurisdiction under the control of Norroy King of Arms, whose title since 1943 is Norroy and Ulster.

William Bruges,
Garter King of Arms.
1420

𝕳𝖊𝖗𝖆𝖑𝖉𝖗𝖞 == 𝕯𝖊𝖘𝖈𝖗𝖎𝖕𝖙𝖎𝖔𝖓 𝖔𝖋 𝕬𝖗𝖒𝖘

In describing Arms the first word indicates the division of the Shield, such as *quarterly* or *parted per pale*. When the Shield is divided, such as quartered or parted, each part is treated as a whole Shield. If the Shield is not divided, the first word will describe the overall metal or colour of the Shield. The Heraldic term giving the colour will be followed by a description of the Shield, naming first the principal ordinary: *Fess, Bend, Chevron*, etc., then the form of the ordinary, such as *Chevron engrailed;* then the colour or metal of the ordinary, such as *A chevron engrailed red*. In order to avoid confusion, we shall use the English terms for colours and metals. After this, the charges are named, such as *roses, roundels, mullets*, etc., giving their position and colour. Then describe the charges, if any, on the ordinary. Where one ordinary is placed over another, it is named last and called *surtout* or *overall*. When this occurs in charges or figures, the first is named and *surmounted by* the last. When a figure or charge is placed on an ordinary, the ordinary is said to be *charged* with the figure or charge. When the main figure is in the center of the Shield, it is not necessary to give its position. Objects of their natural colour are called *proper*. If another colour is used, it must be named. When parts of an animal are of a different colour from that of the body, they are described by making a verb of that particular part, and following the verb with the colour or metal; for example, *a unicorn proper horned gold*. A field strewed with like figures is called *semee*. When a number of like figures are methodically arranged, their number and arrangement must be mentioned, such as *three roses proper in bend;* or *five roses proper, two-one-two in saltire.*

It seems that we have used several Heraldic terms before we have sunk our teeth into the subject. Let us stop a moment and discuss a few of the principle terms used to denote parts of armorial bearings. As we believe that the SCIENCE of Heraldry followed the Norman Conquest, it follows that most of the terms used in Heraldry should be of French origin. We have accustomed ourselves to French words in the nomenclature of the automobile, such as coupe, landau, sedan, tonneau, etc., and in aviation, such as longeron, empennage, aileron, nacelle, etc., so the terms in Heraldry are no more complex if taken in their order.

On the adjacent page is a reproduction of the Arms of Angus John Campbell, 20th Captain of Dunstaffnage, as depicted in Burke's "Landed Gentry." First, what is the difference between Burke's "Landed Gentry" and Burke's "Peerage"? Burke's "Landed Gentry" deals with the class termed Esquires and Gentlemen, who are usually descended from, but not of, the Peerage, Baronetage, or Knightage. Burke's "Peerage" is correctly titled "Peerage, Baronetage, & Knightage." The Peerage of Great Britain consists of

Dukes, Marquesses, Earls, Viscounts and Barons. Peers are also called Nobles, or Lords, and form the Nobility. They are addressed as "My Lord" with the exception of Dukes who are addressed as "Your Grace." Ranking below a Baron, and not in the Nobility, are Baronets or Knights Baronet. This title is most frequently called Bart., but abbreviated Bt. Below a Baronet are the Knights of the various Orders of Great Britain. British subjects who are Knights of foreign or International Orders have no rank or precedence as such in Great Britain. Ranking below the Knights are the Landed Gentry of whom we spoke. Many of the families in the "Landed Gentry" are older than those of the Peerage and frequently have higher *social* position than numerous titled persons.

Concerning the Arms of Angus John Campbell, the entire figure is termed Arms,

A description of the arms quoted from Burke's Landed Gentry: Quarterly; 1st, az. a castle of three towers az., masoned sa. standing on a rock ppr., doors and windows gu.; on the top of the centre tower a cock, on each of the others an eagle or; 2nd, a gyronny of eight or and sa.; 3rd, or, a fess chequy az. and arg.; 4th, gu. a boar's head caboshed or, between a crescent and a spur rowel in fess arg.

Crest — An anchor in pale reversed az.

Motto — Vigilando.

Supporters — Two unicorns arg. horned or, gorged with an antique crown, thereto affixed a chain of the last.

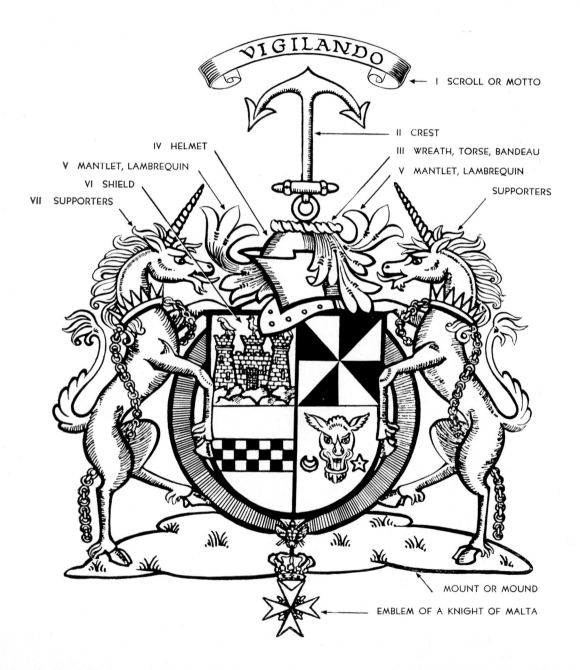

VIGILANDO

I SCROLL OR MOTTO

II CREST

III WREATH, TORSE, BANDEAU

IV HELMET

V MANTLET, LAMBREQUIN

V MANTLET, LAMBREQUIN

VI SHIELD

SUPPORTERS

VII SUPPORTERS

MOUNT OR MOUND

EMBLEM OF A KNIGHT OF MALTA

Arms of
Angus John Campbell
of
Dunstaffnage

as reproduced from
Burke's Landed Gentry

11

or Coat of Arms. The latter expression arises from the practice of embroidering Arms on a surcoat worn over chain armour.

I. SCROLL OR MOTTO: Correctly it is a Motto upon a Scroll. Historians agree that the Motto originated with the War Cry of the Ancients. In the days of hand to hand combat it was the custom for the leader or chief to scream out some short and pithy expression which was echoed through the ranks as they charged upon the foe. This custom served two purposes: First, it gave courage and a spirit of unity to the forces by attacking all at the same time, all with the same words on their tongues; secondly, it struck terror into the foe by the very ferocity of the shout and the attack. This practise was particularly prevalent among the "Wild Hieland" men of Scotland, who in many famous battles, completely overwhelmed in the first minutes of battle vastly numerically superior forces by the utter abandon of their attack. The War Cries of many of the Scottish Clans are not, however, used in their Mottoes, but are retained in their original Gaelic form, and the Motto is frequently an expression referring to some incident in the family history. For example, the Motto of Kirkpatrick of Closeburne comes from an ancestor, Roger de

Kirkpatrick of Closeburne.

Kirkpatrick who was one of the many supporters of Robert the Bruce in his struggle with Red Comyn for the Throne of Scotland. On a fateful day, Bruce's supporters waited outside the Abbey of the Franciscans of Dumfries while Bruce met Comyn inside the Abbey. Bruce, ever adept at infighting, stabbed Comyn and left him fallen. The story goes, that upon reaching his supporters waiting without, Bruce stated "I stabbed him. I'm not sure if mortally." It is said that Kirkpatrick felt that such a momentous thing should not be left in doubt, and cried "I Mak Sicker," whereupon he and Lindsay entered the Abbey and made "Sicker." In memory of this, the Motto of the Kirkpatrick has been I MAK SICKER, and the Crest (#2) is a dexter cubit arm grasping a dagger imbrued (dropping blood) erect.

The Motto is frequently in Latin or French. The Motto of Angus Campbell is VIGILANDO, meaning, according to Burke's Landed Gentry, "by watching." Only in Scotland do we find Mottoes at the top of the Arms. Others appear below the Escutcheon (#6) and not infrequently provide footing for the Supporters (#7). Some Scottish families use two Mottoes, in which case the more important is placed at the top of the Arms.

II. THE CREST: The term Crest is probably the most abused Heraldic term. Never, never under any circumstances refer to a Coat of Arms as a Crest. A Crest is only one small part of the entire armorial bearing. Crests came into use during the Age of Chivalry before the use of the surcoat. Their purpose was to make the wearer readily distinguishable to friend or foe in the melee of battle. On such occasions a shield or escutcheon (#6) was not visible from the rear, and if the going were heavy, it was probably rather difficult to distinguish from any position, whereas a Crest mounted atop the helmet (#4) could be seen and recognized immediately. Crests have been handed down from generation to generation, and have become symbolic of the families to whom they belong. New Crests have been adopted by new branches of old families and by new families obtaining Arms. Some Arms will have two and even three Crests, a custom upon which Grant rather pithily observes "Is illogical, as a person has only one head, and therefore could not wear two helmets." Arms of ladies have no Crests.

The Crest of Angus Campbell is *An anchor in pale reversed (upside down) blue.*

III. THE W R E A T H — TORSE — BANDEAU: The Wreath appears to be a roll of two colours composed of the main metal and the main tincture of the escutcheon (#6). Actually, it was formed by twisting two skeins of silk together. The Wreath was used to fasten the Crest and the Lambrequin (#5) to the helmet (#4). In Heraldry, Crests are frequently shown issuing from a Crown, Coronet, or Chapeau, in which case a Wreath is not shown.

IV. THE HELMET: As we all know, the Helmet was originally a piece of armour worn over the head, having an opening in front called the visor. There was also the beaked type upon which the beaver could be raised. In Heraldry, the metal from which the helmet is made, its type, and its position denote the station of the bearer. The helmet of Sovereign Princes is gold placed full front view, and is the grated type with six bars. The helmet of all degrees of Peerage (Duke, Marquess, Earl, Viscount and Baron) is silver trimmed with gold, placed in profile, and is the grated type with five bars. The helmet of Baronets and Knights is made of polished steel, placed full front view, with the beaver raised or open. The helmet of Esquires and Gentlemen is of polished steel, placed in profile, with the beaver closed. Notice that the helmet shown is in profile and closed, indicating the bearer to be of the rank of Gentleman or Esquire. (To those who recognize the Emblem of the Knights of Malta — that Order carries no precedence in Great Britain.)

V. LAMBREQUIN — MANTLET — MANTLING: In Heraldry, the Lambrequin is depicted as scroll work or plumage, and has great value as a decoration in more simple or severe Arms. Originally it was worn with armour to serve as a protection to the armour and the wearer. One can well imagine that a hot summer's sun could make a helmet untenable. Lambrequins were frequently ripped to shreds in battle; in fact, an extremely tattered one was borne with great pride. The colours of the Lambrequin are taken from the principal metal and tincture of the Escutcheon.

VI. SHIELD — FIELD — ESCUTCHEON: This is the main part of the Coat of Arms. (For divisions of the Shield see the center figure on *page 17.*)

In Heraldry, dexter and sinister are used in reference to the sides of an object. Dexter means right, and sinister means left, but remember that on a Shield, the sides are considered from the position of the person wearing the Arms, or reverse to the observer; thus dexter corresponds to your left, and sinister to your right. This is not true of figures.

This Shield is divided quarterly (into four equal parts). The first quarter is coloured blue, and upon it is emblazoned a castle of three towers blue and masoned black, standing on a rock gray, doors and windows red. Atop the center tower a cock gold, on each of the others an eagle gold. This is probably symbolic of the famous and romantic Dunstaffnage Castle. This castle is situated at the point of a peninsula in Loch (lake) Etive. At one time the peninsula was an island called Archinche, and was the seat of the Dalriadic Kings. On this spot was kept the Lia Fail, or Stone of Destiny, upon which Scottish Kings were crowned. At about 850 A.D. King Kenneth MacAlpin moved the Stone of Destiny to Skone.

Dunstaffnage, a part of Lorn, was among the vast holdings of Alexander of Ergadia who built the existing castle about 1250. Both he and his son, John of Lorn, were bitterly opposed to King Robert the Bruce who destroyed them in 1308. The titles and lands of Lorn passed into the hands of the Stewarts. The Campbells wanted Lorn and when Sir John Stewart, Lord of Lorn, was murdered, Colin Campbell, 1st Earl of Argyle, appointed Dugald Mor Campbell captain of Dunstaffnage Castle. The Campbells still have it; the present holder is the 20th hereditary captain.

The second, or sinister chief quarter of

the Escutcheon contains a gyronny of eight (gold and black) for Campbell.

The third, or dexter base quarter, is gold with a Fess Chequey (blue and silver) for Stewart.

The fourth, or sinister base quarter, is red with a boar's head caboshed (full face with no neck) of gold, between a crescent and mullet (rowell or five pointed star) pierced, both in Fess (horizontally across the center of the quarter) both silver.

VII. THE SUPPORTERS: These are figures on either side of a Shield, apparently supporting it. They are frequently pairs, as in this case, and usually two, but in some cases one is used. In England, they may be borne only by the Nobility or to Knights Grand Cross of the various orders of Knighthood. In Scotland, the Lyon King of Arms has the power to grant them to Chiefs of Clans, or gentlemen who can prove their use prior to 1672, as well as to Peers. This honorable gentleman's Arms are adorned with Supporters by right of the ancient proprietorship of his line, and by his captaincy of a considerable branch of the very large Clan Campbell. These Supporters are described as two unicorns (silver) horned (gold) gorged (meaning collared) with an antique crown, thereto affixed a chain of the last (gold). The uni-

corn thus adorned is also the Supporter of the Royal Arms of Scotland.

Members of Noble families or Clans difference their Arms from those of the title holder, chief, or captain. In England, marks of difference or cadency, *see page 19*, to denote relation, are added at the wish of the member, but in Scotland each son or cadet must *matriculate* his Arms at the Court of the Lyon King of Arms. The Lyon Office worked out a Scheme of Cadency where bordures are added, then further differenced in the next generation by *investing* and *engrailing, see page 19*, the bordure, etc. This Scheme of Cadency is a study in itself, and is, we believe, beyond the scope of this book. Daughters do not difference Arms, but bear their fathers' on a lozenge shaped Shield with no Crest.

After discussing honourable ordinaries and charges, let us give a moment to Charges of Abatement or Abatements of Honour. They are the source of the expression "Blots on the Escutcheon." Authorities agree that no Arms, which are theoretically marks of honour, would be displayed if so charged. We can find no proof that such abated Arms were ever borne. There are, however, marks of abatement for illegitimacy which were borne by illegitimate sons of Royalty. In England the abatement for this is a *baton sinister;* in Scot-

BATON.
Arms of Fitzroy,
Duke of Grafton.

15

land, a *bordure compony*. A practise used first by the Normans was to add the prefix "Fitz" to a given name, and thus form the surname of a *natural* son of Royalty; for example, the Arms of Fitzroy, Duke of Grafton.

Beside National, Royal, and Family Arms, there are countless commercial Arms granted in Great Britain. Examples of National Arms are shown on *pages 69 and 70*, and examples of Commercial Arms on *pages 71 through 74*. In the United States, business concerns adopt Arms belonging to families of Europe, or have Arms made to suit their tastes. The Arms of the Cadillac Motor Car are those of Cadillac, French explorer and founder of Detroit. The Arms of the Buick have been changed in shape from year to year, but all have contained, in some form, the Chequey blue and silver, of the Stewarts of Scotland. The Arms on the Frazer Car are the exact Arms of Sir Simon Frazer, Baron Lovat of Scotland, even to the Motto "Je Suis Pret" (I Am Ready). 1950 finds even the Ford Car sporting an Escutcheon.

Most Fraternal Orders have Arms or Badges, and many of the Greek letter Fraternity and Sorority Arms are quite elaborate.

On the matter of who may display Arms — the answer depends entirely upon one's citizenship and viewpoint. In the United States, anyone may legally display any Arms he chooses. There are neither laws nor registry regarding armorial bearings. True, there is a registry for tademarks, and a trademark may be an Heraldic design, but generally speaking, there is no registry of Arms. There is nothing to prevent anyone in the United States from displaying any personal or family Arms. For example, the Frazer of Lovat Arms on the Frazer Car correctly belong only to Sir Simon Frazer of Lovat. It is, however, neither correct nor in good taste to assume or display the Arms of the holder of some foreign title merely because one has the same surname. Families of Great Britain have original Arms which will be present in some form in the Arms of most of the descendents; for example, the gold and black gyronny of eight for Campbell, the silver and blue Chequey of the Stewarts, and a boar's head erased for Gordon. An Escutcheon bearing these original Arms may correctly be displayed by anyone of that name. They may not, however, correctly use the Supporters, Crests, or Mottoes, as these belong only to the title holder. A gentleman's helmet and elaborate plumage (lambrequin) may be added to relieve the severity of a simple Shield — but in the assumption of armorial bearings, one may do as his fancy dictates.

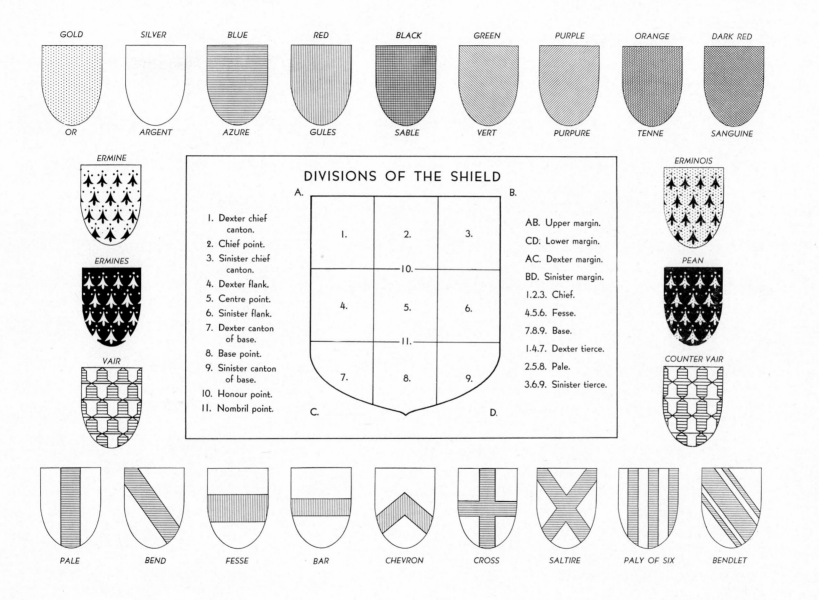

GOLD SILVER BLUE RED BLACK GREEN PURPLE ORANGE DARK RED

OR ARGENT AZURE GULES SABLE VERT PURPURE TENNE SANGUINE

ERMINE

ERMINES

VAIR

ERMINOIS

PEAN

COUNTER VAIR

DIVISIONS OF THE SHIELD

A. B.

1. Dexter chief canton.
2. Chief point.
3. Sinister chief canton.
4. Dexter flank.
5. Centre point.
6. Sinister flank.
7. Dexter canton of base.
8. Base point.
9. Sinister canton of base.
10. Honour point.
11. Nombril point.

AB. Upper margin.
CD. Lower margin.
AC. Dexter margin.
BD. Sinister margin.
1.2.3. Chief.
4.5.6. Fesse.
7.8.9. Base.
1.4.7. Dexter tierce.
2.5.8. Pale.
3.6.9. Sinister tierce.

C. D.

PALE BEND FESSE BAR CHEVRON CROSS SALTIRE PALY OF SIX BENDLET

17

Fig.
1. A Cross Pierced or Perforated.
2. A Cross Voided: When a part of an ordinary is left open to the field, it is termed *Voided;* for example, in *Figure* 2, the field is silver, and the cross is red. What it actually amounts to in this case is that it is outlined in red.
3. A Cross Surmounted: One cross placed over another; in this case, a cross red surmounted by a cross gold.
4. A Cross Couped and Voided: A cross is an honourable ordinary and normally extends to the edges of the shield. In this case it is *couped* (cut off) so that the arms do not reach the edges of the shield. It is also *voided,* as explained in *Figure* 2.
5. A Cross Couped, Fimbriated: An ordinary with a narrow border of a different tincture is termed *Fimbriated*.
6. A Cross Quartered — Quarter Pierced.
7. A Cross Watered.

Fig.
8. A Cross Interlaced.
9. A Cross Quarterly Quartered.
10. A Cross Pometty: Knobbed at both ends.
11. A Cross Fleury — Flory: Adorned with Fleur de Lys.
12. A Cross Quarterly Quartered Fleury.
13. A Cross Crossed: If *couped,* termed a *cross crosslet*.
14. A Cross Nowey.
15. A Cross Degraded: A cross ending in steps.
16. A Cross Fusilly: A cross made of *fusils, see Page* 30, *Figure* 16.
17. A Cross Couped and Fitched — Fitchy — Fichee: The lower branch pointed, so that it may be fixed into the ground.
18. A Cross Humetty: A term applied to ordinaries which are cut off so they do not touch the edge of the shield, but are not *couped* (cut in a straight line).

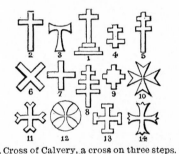

Top row shields: 1 2 3 4 5 6 7 8 9

THE FILE or LABEL,
Mark of the eldest son.

THE CRESCENT,
The second son's mark

THE MULLET,
The third son's mark.

THE MARTLET,
The fourth son's mark.

THE ANNULET,
The fifth son's mark.

THE FLEUR-DE-LYS,
The sixth son's mark.

THE ROSE,
The seventh son's mark.

THE CROSS MOLINE,
The eight son's mark.

THE OCTOFOIL,
The ninth son's mark.

MARKS OF CADENCY

Distinguishing marks applied to a Coat-of-Arms

1, Cross of Calvery, a cross on three steps. 2, Latin Cross, a cross the transverse beam of which is placed at one-third the distance from the top of the perpendicular portion, supposed to be the form of cross on which Christ suffered. 3, Tau Cross, (so called from being formed like the Greek letter **r**, tau), or cross of St. Anthony, one of the most ancient forms of the cross. 4, Cross of Lorraine. 5, Patriarchal Cross. 6, St. Andrew's Cross, the form of cross on which St. Andrew, the national saint of Scotland, is said to have suffered. 7, Greek Cross, or cross of St. George. the national saint of England, the red cross which appears on British flags. 8, Papal Cross. 9, Cross nowy quadrat, that is, having a square expansion in the center. 10, Maltese Cross, formed of four arrow-heads meeting at the points; the badge of the Knights of Malta. 11, Cross fourchée or forked. 12, Cross pattée or formée. 13, Cross potent or Jerusalem Cross. 14, Cross fleury, from the fleur de lis at its ends.

Engrailed
Invected
Ondé - wavy
Nebulé
Indented
Dancette (3 Indentations)
Embattled
Potent
Raguly
Dovetailed
Rayonne
Nowy
Escartelé
Angled
Bevelled

LINES USED TO DIVIDE THE SHIELD.

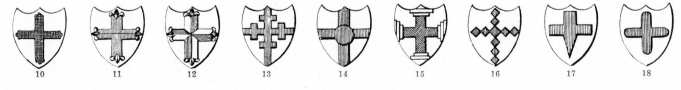

Bottom row shields: 10 11 12 13 14 15 16 17 18

1. A Cross Couped and Voided: *See Page* 19, *Figures* 2 *and* 4.
2. A Cross Potent.
3. A Cross Double Fitched Each Arm: Each arm double pointed.
4. A Cross Pommelled: *See pommelled in dictionary.*
5. A Cross Moline: The shape of the arm ends is taken from the *Fer de Moline, see Fer de Moline in dictionary.*
6. A Cross Mascle Voided; At Each Point a Plate: A cross made up of *voided mascles.* A *plate* is a silver *roundel. See Page* 25, *Figure* 38.
7. A Cross Fusil: The ends of the arms have a shape of a *fusil. See fusil, Page* 25, *Figure* 40.
8. A Cross Triparted Fleury.
9. A Cross Anserated: At each point two gooseheads addorsed (*back to back*).
10. Parted per Bend.
11. Parted per Pale.
12. Parted per Fess.
13. Parted per Saltire.
14. Parted per Bend Sinister: A reverse *bend* that goes from *sinister chief* to *dexter base.*
15. Quarterly or Parted per Quarter.
16. Parted in Three per Pale.
17. Parted in Three per Fess.
18. Parted in Three Bendways.
19. Parted in Three per Bend Sinister.
20. Parted in Three per Mantle.
21. Parted in Three per Gusset.

22. Parted in Three per Traverse Dexter.
23. Parted in Three Gyron Bend Sinisterways.
24. Triparted in Pale.
25. Parted in Three Round Gyrones.
26. Parted in Four Stepways.
27. Parted in Four Round Gyrones.
28. A Gyronny of Six.
29. A Gyronny of Eight.
30. Parted Champagne. *See champagne in dictionary.*
31. Parted per Fess per Pale: *Note difference from Figure* 41.
32. Parted Quarterly per Pale in Base.
33. Parted per Champagne Concaved.
34. Parted per Bend Crenelle or Bend Embattled.
35. Parted per Fess Embattled Grady.
36. Parted per Chevron.
37. Parted per Cour: One Dancette. *See Page* 19 *on lines.*
38. Parted per Gore: *See gore in dictionary.*
39. Parted per Gusset: A triangular piece of chain-mail between plates of armour.
40. Parted per Pale and Chevron Counter Changed.
41. Parted per Pale and Fess: *Note difference from Figure* 31.
42. A Counter Paly of Three Parted per Fess (*Counter Changed*).
43. Parted per Pale; First Quarterly.
44. Parted per Pale and Fess of Six Counter Changed.
45. A Paly and Fess of Nine Counter Changed.

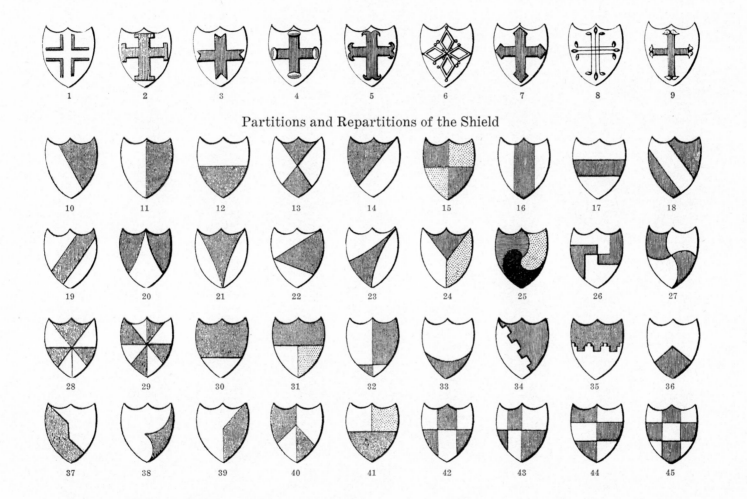

Partitions and Repartitions of the Shield

Fig.

1. A Double Tressure Counter Fleury: Tressure — double lines going around a shield at the same distance from its edge; in this case a double tressure ornamented with Fleurs de Lys, with the points running alternately in a contrary direction.

2. B r o u c h a n t : Placed over, overlying, or surmounted.

3. Counter Changed per Pale: When the tinctures of a shield or charge are interchanged in two positions.

4. A Chief Lowered, A Bend Abaisse: *For Chief Lowered, see Page* 23, *Figure* 5; *For Abaisse, see dictionary.*

5. Roses Aspersed: Aspersed means semee, powdered, strewed, sprinkled with.

6. Bezantee — Bezanted: Semee with bezants. *See roundels in dictionary.*

7. Billetty: Semee with billets. *See billets in dictionary.*

8. Cheque — Chequee — Chequey — Checky: Alternate squares of metal and colour or fur.

9. Checquer: Smaller squares than Cheque.

10. Three Couple Closes Braced: A Couple close is a diminutive of the chevron. *See chevron in dictionary. Braced, brased,* and *brazed* refer to figures of the same form interlacing each other.

11. Two Serpents Complexed.

12. A Cordon: A silver cord which encircles the arms of a widow.

13. Three Annulets Cojoined Braced: *See dictionary.*

14. Corded: Bound with a cord. This term is used when the cord is of a different tincture from that of the object bound.

15. Three Arrows Banded: Tied with a cord.

16. Two Stalks of Corn in Saltire.

17. A Stalk of Corn Bladed Three: *See bladed in dictionary.*

18. A Rose.

19. Blazing — Ablaze: Burning, afire.

20. A Dart with a Barb: *See barb in dictionary.*

Fig.

21. A Rose Barbed. *See barbed in the dictionary.*

22. A Canton: A small square figure placed in the dexter chief corner of the shield.

23. An Escutcheon of Pretence: A small escutcheon bearing the arms of a wife who is an heiress, surmounting at the fess point the arms of her husband. *See inescutcheon in the dictionary.*

24. The First Quarter.

25. A Fret: *See fret in dictionary.*

26. An Orle: An open inescutcheon one half the width of a bordure.

27. A Pile: A triangular figure shaped like a wedge.

28. V o i d e r : A subordinate ordinary formed by curved lines placed opposite each other.

29. A Flask: One half a *Voider.*

30. Flanch: One half a *Flask.*

31. A Tressure: A diminutive of an *orle.*

32. Chaplet: *See chaplet in dictionary.*

33. Annulet: *See annulet in dictionary.*

34. Trefoile: Three leaves, also the shamrock of Ireland.

35. Quarterfoile: Four leaves.

36. Cinquefoile: Five leaves — occasionally used to denote a rose.

37. A Rostre — Rustre: A lozenge pierced with a circle. *See Figure* 39.

38. A Mascle: *See mascle in dictionary.*

39. A Lozenge: *See lozenge in dictionary.*

40. A Fusil: *See fusil in dictionary.*

41. A Chapeau or Cap of Maintenance: A cap of dignity formed of crimson or scarlet velvet lined and turned up with ermine, borne by sovereign princes.

42. Cap of State: Civic Cap. *See Cap of State in dictionary.*

43. A Hand Aversant: Turned away from.

44. A Hand Apalmy.

45. A Lion Salient: Salient is a position similar to *rampant* except that both hind paws are on the ground, and the body is not as erect — said by some to be a leaping position.

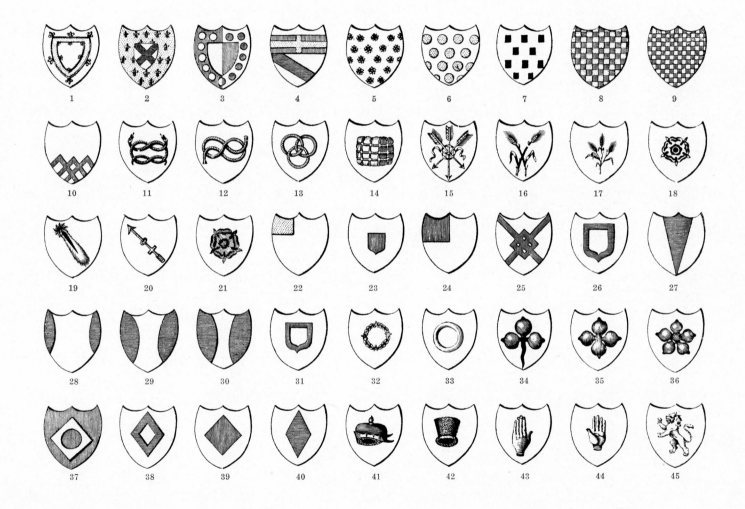

Page 27 gives examples of various figures in different positions which will be described below, and in the dictionary.

Fig.

1. A Lion Couchant: A position of an animal lying down, with the head uplifted.

2. A Lion Passant Guardant: *Passant* refers to a profile view of a beast standing with one forepaw uplifted; *Guardant* denotes that the head is facing the observer, regardless of the position of the body.

3. A Lion Dormant: Lying down as if sleeping.

4. A Lion Rampant Reguardant: *Rampant* refers to a profile view of the beast standing erect on the sinister (left) hind leg, with both forelegs elevated, the dexter (right) above the sinister; *Reguardant* refers only to the position of the head, and means *turned backwards*.

5. A Lion Rampant: *See Figure 4 above.*

6. A Lion Rampant Guardant: *See Rampant Figure 4; Guardant Figure 2.*

7. Issuant: Coming out of. This term frequently used in describing Crests, where a figure issues from a Crown, etc. *See Page 37, Figure 16.*

8. Jessant: This also means coming out of, but refers to figures coming out of a field or parts thereof. *See Page 35, Figure 10.*

9. Naissant: Also means coming out of, but refers only to figures emerging from an ordinary; in this case a fess.

10. A Lion Assise or Sejant: The latter term is more frequently used, and refers to an animal sitting on its hind legs.

11. A Lion Contournee or Cotournee: Turned around. In Heraldry, figures ordinarily face the dexter (right) side of the shield. If for some reason, the charge is placed facing the sinister (left) side, it is termed *contournee.*

12. A Lion Rampant Cowarded: In all positions except *dormant,* an animal's tail is shown up; if it is shown drooping or between the hind legs, it is termed *cowarded.*

13. A Lion Rampant Battonnee: Carrying a baton.

Fig.

14. A Lion Rampant Bicapitated: Two headed. In the case of bicapitated birds, the heads are placed back to back, or *addorsed. See Figure 18.*

15. Bicorporated: Two figures having a common head.

16. Counter Passant: *Counter* means two like figures, one above the other, facing in opposite directions.

17. Two Lions Combatant: Figures *rampant* facing each other, as if in combat.

18. Two Lions Rampant Addorsed or Addorssee: Back to back.

19. A Lamb Accule: A position similar to rampant, but the paws or hoofs pointed downward.

20. A Bull's Head and Neck Couped: Cut off in a straight line.

21. A Wolf Rampant: *See Figure 4 for rampant.*

22. Two Squirrels Addorsed: Back to back.

23. Two Salmon Hauriant Addorssee: *Hauriant* is a term of position applied only to fish. It has the same meaning as *erect. See dictionary.*

24. Two Salmon Hauriant Affrontee or Affronted: Face to face, but not *combatant.*

25. Two Salmon Counter Naiant: *Naiant* means swimming, but is applied to any fish in a horizontal position. *For counter see Figure 16.*

26. Counter Salient: *Salient* is a position similar to *rampant,* except that both hind paws are on the ground, and the position of the body is not as erect, but more in a leaping position. *For counter see Figure 16.* Animals *counter salient* are shown as a *saltire* cross.

27. Two Lambs Ambulant: Walking.

28. Two Stags Counter Trippant: *Trippant* is the motion of a deer between running and walking. *For counter see Figure 16.*

29. A Stag Arrete: A position of the head the same as *guardant,* but the gaze is supposed to be more intent. This term is used with reference to the deer family, and is sometimes termed *at gaze.*   (Continued on Page 28)

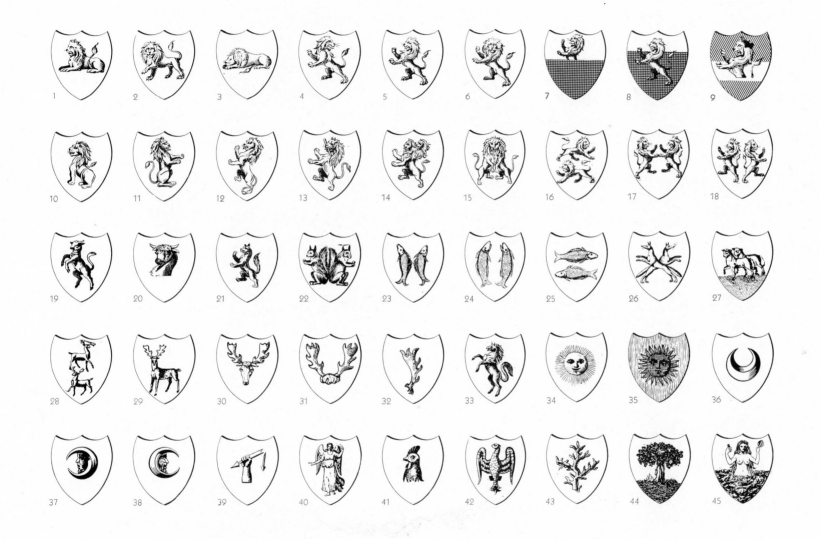

(*Continued from Page* 26)

Fig.
30. A Stag's Head Caboched, Caboshed, Cabossed, Cabossee: A beast's head full faced, with no part of the neck showing.
31. Antlers.
32. An Antler.
33. A Horse Accule: *See Figure* 19.
34. A Moon in Her Complement: Heraldic term for a full moon.
35. A Moon Adumbrated or in Her Detriment: A moon eclipsed or overshadowed.
36. Crescent or Cressent: A crescent with the horns turned upward.
37. Increscent or Incressent: A moon in her first quarter, the horns turned to the dexter side of the shield.
38. Decrescent or Decressent: A moon in her wane, or third quarter, the horns turned toward the sinister side of the shield.
39. A Lance Biparted: Broken into two pieces, with both pieces shown.
40. An Angel Habited: Clothed.
41. A Cock Barbed and Crested: *See dictionary for both terms.*
42. Allerion: An eagle displayed without beak or feet. *See displayed in dictionary.*
43. A Branch Raguly: *See dictionary.*
44. A Tree Accrued: Growing. *Accrued afresh* refers to a stump or fallen log growing.
45. A Mermaid Assurgant: A figure rising from the water.

Page 29 shows two forms used in preparing Heraldic Figures. Those on the left are the outline, or painters' form; those on the right are the engravers' form, where intricate shading is used. This represents Heraldic Art at its finest. Only great skill and meticulous care can produce beautiful and correct engravings.

Fig.
1. A griffin's head erased.
2. A lion's head cabossed.
3. A doe's head and neck erased.
4. A lion's head and neck erased.

Fig.
5. A bicapitated eagle displayed.
6. A bull's head and neck erased.
7. A demi-griffin rampant.
8. A mountain lion's head cabossed.
9. A demi-eagle with wings displayed.
10. A dexter gamb erased and clenched.
11. A martlet close.
12. A lion passant reguardant.

Page 30 contains ten examples of family arms, two of which have supporters. They will be used as examples for terms in the dictionary. The center figure is the Seal of the Sovereign State of Illinois. The four remaining figures are described below.

Fig.
6. A dexter gamb erased, clenching a key bend sinisterways, therefrom hanging a chain.
7. Issuant from flames, a demi-eagle bicapitated displayed.
10. A fish head hauriant couped, between two plumes erect.
11. A dexter gamb erased, clenching a spear with a pennon; the pennon charged with a bicapitated eagle displayed.

See Page 31.
Fig.
1. A wivern clenching a glove in its beak.
2. A bee displayed.
3. A mullet.
4. A torteaux. *See roundels in dictionary.*
5. A lion's head and neck erased, gorged.
6. A griffin passant segreant, ducally gorged.
10. A demi-lion rampant; its dexter paw clutching a sword bend sinisterways.
11. A staff of wheat and a broken lance in saltire, surmounted by a crescent.
12. A wolverine passant.
13. A stag lodged, surmounted by a picket fence.
14. Two swords in saltire banded at the fess point, with a key hanging therefrom.
15. A falcon, its wings disclosed, and its dexter claw resting on a shield couchee.

1

2

3

4

5

6

7

8

9

10

11

12

VIRTUS ET SPES

STATE SOVEREIGNTY
NATIONAL UNION

[Illinois]

FORTITER

PER MARE PER TERRAS

1   2   3   4   5

6   7   10   11

12   13   14   15   16

INTEGER VITA

J.T.Abbott
Abbeville.
Darlington 1860

AGE OFFICIUM TUUM

DIEU ET MON DROIT

1 2 3 4 5 6

7 8 9

10 11 12 13 14 15

TOUJOURS PRESTE

SHANID A BOO

1 2 3 4 5
6 7 8 9 10 11
12 13 14 15 16

See Page 32.
Fig.

6. A trefoile between two wings erect.

7. A dexter hand couped at the wrist clenching a key in bend sinister.

8. A globe of the earth ensigned by a three masted ship in full sail, pennons flying.

9. A pheasant lying on its back being attacked by a hawk.

10. A horse's head and neck couped, armoured and bridled.

11. A key erect surmounted by a sword and crosier in saltire.

See Page 34.
Fig.

1. On a chapeau, a lion statant guardant.

2. A dexter hand couped at the wrist erect, clutching a chaplet.

3. A griffin's head erased, in its beak a serpent.

4. On a mount, a greyhound sejant.

5. A trumpet fessways, surmounted by a swan rising.

6. On a chapeau turned up ermine, an eagle's head and neck erased.

7. The Arms of Cheney, giving an example of a canton ermine, surmounting one of six lions rampant, placed in pile 3, 2, and 1.

10. A sword erect enfilated by a boar's head erased.

11. A cony being attacked by an eagle.

12. A demi-bowman unvested.

13. Two arms couped at the shoulders, vambraced, embowed, holding a Lochober Axe bend sinisterways.

Fig.

14. A dexter cubit arm holding an anchor erect.

15. On a table, a falcon close.

See Page 35.
Fig.

1. A stag's head and neck couped, between the antlers a cross pattee.

2. A man's head erased, barbed, and enfiled on a spear erect.

3. A caltrap embrued.

4. A dove close, perched on a fallen log.

5. A figure of a man barbed, vested and close girt, couped at the knees, wearing a chaplet; his dexter arm embowed, holding aloft a ring.

6. A stag's head and neck erased.

8. A dexter cubit arm, vested and cuffed, clenching a branch raguly bend sinisterways.

9. A crane's head and neck couped, with a serpent in its beak.

11. A dexter hand couped at the wrist, erect, holding a fusil.

12. An eagle's head and neck erased, holding a mullet in its beak.

14. A fox sejant reguardant, with its dexter paw on a lozenge in bend, all on a mount.

15. On a mount, a horse sejant, facing a tree accrued.

16. A stork, supporting with its dexter claw, an anchor.

17. A stag passant.

18. On a mount, a peacock holding a rose slipped and leaved.

19. A sinister hand apaumy couped fesswise, supporting a falcon close.

LE MIEUX QUE JE PUIS

Cheney

Clarence Chapman Cheney

7

QUIS SEPARABIT
MDCCLXXXIII
fidelite est de Dieu

8

AVISÉ LA FIN

Alfred C. Kennedy!

9

1

2

3

4

5

6

10

11

12

13

14

15

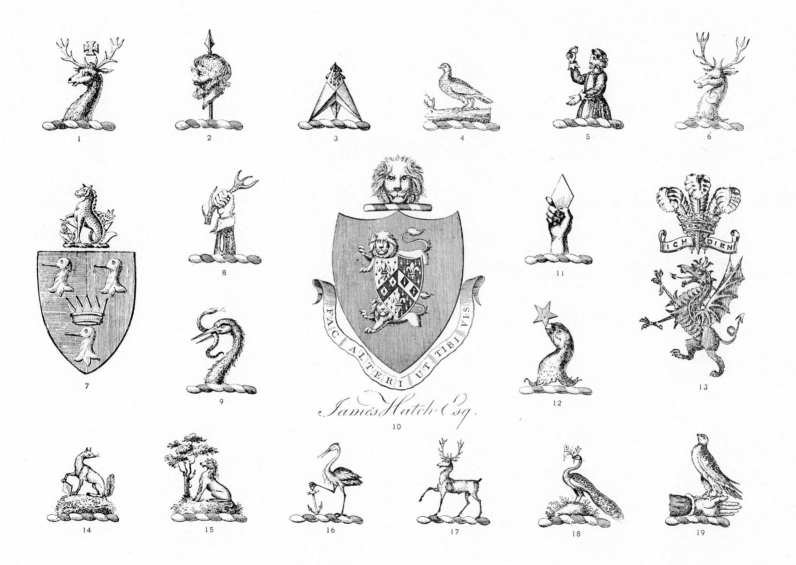

James Hatch Esq.

See Page 37.
Fig.

1. A hawk close.
2. A lion rampant, between its paws a diadem.
3. A lion passant, with its dexter paw atop a Fleur de Lys.
4. A wolf passant.
5. A lion rampant.
6. On a mount, a hawk with wings displayed, ducally gorged.
7. A spotted leopard sejant, with its dexter paw raised to support the staff of a British ensign.
8. A bear statant, gorged, chained, and muzzled.
9. A rhinoceros ambulant.
10. A griffin sejant, its dexter claw raised clutching a sword in bend sinister, the sword enfilated with a man's head barbed and couped.
11. A demi-greyhound rampant, gorged, between two wings erect.
12. A lion rampant reguardant; its dexter paw clutching a torch aflame bend sinisterways.
14. A griffin rampant, clutching between its claws, a sol. *See sol in dictionary.*
15. A doe's head and neck couped, between two roses barbed; the stems slipped and leaved.

Fig.

16. Issuant from a diadem, a demi-swan rising, holding in its beak an arrow bendways point downward.
17. A griffin passant reguardant, wings segreant.
18. Issuant from a diadem, a dexter cubit arm clutching three arrows.
19. Atop a ducal crown, a falcon close.
20. A wolf rampant reguardant.
21. Issuant from a mural crown, a lioness gorged ducally.

See Page 38.

2. A knight vambraced and mounted on a horse courant; his dexter arm embowed, holding a sword erect; bearing on his helmet as a crest, a demi-lion rampant; the chest of his armour bearing a shield charged with a lion rampant; the barding of his horse bearing four shields charged each with a lion rampant.
3. A staff of big wheat.
4. On a mount, five staffs of wheat.
5. A horse passant; its dexter leg supporting a Latin Cross.
11. On a mount of wheat, a garb of wheat.
12. On a stump, accrued afresh a squirrel sejant.

37

1

2

3

4

5

6

7

Sir George Stewart of Grandtully, Bar.ᵗ

8

9

10

11

13

12

14

PRO REGE ET REPVBLICA

MISERERE·MEI·DEVS

2

Lyon King of arms.

MISERERE·MEI·DEVS

3

CORONET AND SHIELD OF GARTER KING OF ARMS.

1

TUTUS PROMPTO ANIMO

AUS CHAMBERLAIN.

40

Fig.

1. A demi-lion rampant crowned with a diadem.
2. Issuant from a ducal crown, a demi-lion rampant charged on the sinister shoulder with a crescent.
3. A lion's head and neck erased, crowned with a diadem.
4. A lion statant guardant cowarded.
5. A lion accule, gorged.
6. A lion passant, in its dexter paw a Fleur de Lys.
7. A lion's head and neck erased.
8. A lion rampant, between its paws an hour-glass.
9. A demi-lion rampant.
10. Issuant from a mural crown, a demi-lion rampant; in its dexter paw a battleaxe.
11. A lion's head and neck erased between two sprigs of whortleberry disposed in orle, surmounted by two cross crosslets fitchee in saltire.
12. A demi-lion rampant supporting a spear erect with a pennon.
13. A demi-lion rampant guardant, between its paws a Fleur de Lys.
14. A lion rampant supporting a scroll.
15. A lion sejant, its dexter paw raised to support a battleaxe in pale.
16. Behind a lion couchant guardant, a partly disclosed sol.
17. Atop an embattled tower, a lion sejant; its dexter paw raised, resting on an anchor bendways.
18. A lion rampant, holding in its dexter paw a sceptre erect; its sinister forepaw and dexter hindpaw on a globe of the earth.
19. Four lions passant guardant.
20. Atop an embattled crown, a lion rampant guardant, supporting a Latin Cross.
21. Atop a Sovereign Crown, a lion statant guardant, crowned Royally.
22. A demi-lion rampant, between its paws a chaplet.
23. Atop a chapeau, a lion statant, with its tail extended fessways.
24. A lion statant.
25. A lion sejant, its dexter paw resting on a Cross Patonce.
26. Issuant from a ducal crown, a demi-lion displayed.

Fig.

27. Issuant from a tower, an anchor bend sinisterways, surmounted by a lion's head and neck erased.
28. A demi-lion rampant; on its shoulder a chevron charged with three escallops; between its paws a shield charged with a martlet.
29. Three lions passant.
30. A demi-lion rampant, gorged with a collar charged with three roundels, holding between its paws a mascle enfilated with a serpent in fess.
31. A lion rampant.
32. A demi-lion rampant, between its paws an escallop.
33. A demi-lion rampant, holding in its paws a long stemmed rose slipped, fructed, and leaved; a serpent entwined around its body.
34. A lion's head caboshed.
35. A lion rampant, holding in its dexter paw a sceptre erect; its sinister forepaw and dexter hindpaw on a globe of the earth.
36. A lion rampant, gorged with a diadem, and chained.
37. A lion rampant, holding between its paws, a saltire.
38. A demi-lion rampant, its dexter paw holding a mullet.
39. A lion rampant surmounting four battleaxes, disposed 2 and 2 addorsed, forming a saltire; all on a mount.
40. A lion rampant, holding between its paws a diadem.
41. On a mount, a demi-lion rampant; its sinister paw resting on an escallop; its dexter paw holding a thistle slipped, leaved, and fructed.
42. Issuant from a mural crown, a demi-lion rampant holding a key erect.
43. A lion rampant; in its dexter paw a Fleur de Lys bend sinisterways.
44. Atop an embattled tower, a lion sejant; its dexter paw raised, resting on an anchor bendways.
45. A lion rampant guardant.
46. A lion passant guardant; in its dexter paw a sword erect.

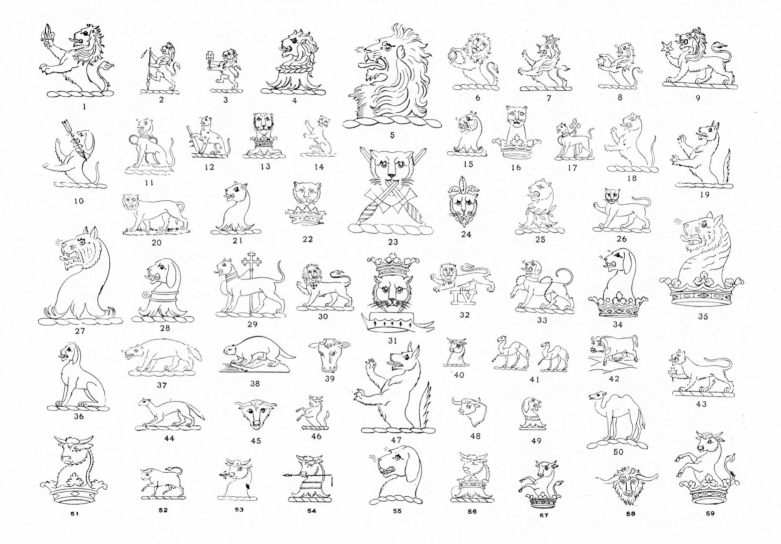

1. A demi-lion rampant, clutching in its dexter paw, a Fleur de Lys.
2. A lion rampant, supporting a lance biparted erect.
3. A lion rampant clutching a cross pattee fitched.
4. A lion's head and neck erased, gorged with a wreath.
5. A lion's head couped.
6. A demi-lion rampant guardant, between its paws a crescent.
7. A demi-lion rampant crowned ducally.
8. A demi-lion rampant, holding between its paws, a mullet.
9. A lion passant, its dexter paw holding a mullet pierced.
10. A demi-talbot rampant gorged, holding in its mouth, an arrow.
11. A mountain lion sejant, gorged ducally and chained.
12. A mountain lion sejant, bezantee; its dexter paw resting on a baton in bend.
13. A lion's head and neck erased guardant, gorged ducally.
14. A cat o' mountain salient, sejant, guardant.
15. A mountain lion's head and neck erased.
16. Issuant from a diadem, a mountain lion's head guardant, erased.
17. A mountain lion statant, gorged and chained to, and surmounting a cross crosslet fitched.
18. A demi-mountain lion rampant.
19. A demi-wolf rampant.
20. A mountain lion guardant, ambulant, and cowarded.
21. A mountain lion's head and neck erased.
22. Above a ducal crown, a mountain lion's head cabossed.
23. A mountain lion's head cabossed, enfiled through the mouth by two swords in saltire.
24. A Fleur de Lys surmounted by a mountain lion's head caboshed.
25. A mountain lion's head and neck erased, gorged with laurel.
26. A mountain lion passant guardant.
27. A mountain lion's head and neck erased.

28. A talbot's head and neck erased, gorged.
29. A mountain lion statant, gorged and chained to, and surmounting, a cross crosslet fitched.
30. A lion passant guardant, charged on the neck with a cross patonce.
31. Atop a Cap of Maintenance turned up ermine, a mountain lion's head caboshed, crowned with a diadem.
32. A lion passant guardant atop a Roman numeral IV.
33. A talbot passant, gorged and chained.
34. Issuant from a ducal crown, a talbot's head and neck.
35. Issuant from a diadem, a tiger's head and neck.
36. A talbot sejant.
37. A brock statant.
38. On a mount, an otter statant.
39. A cow's head caboched.
40. A bull's head and neck couped.
41. Dromedaries passant.
42. A water buffalo courant.
43. A lioness passant, clutching in its dexter paw a cross moline fitched.
44. A fox statant.
45. An oxen head caboshed.
46. A demi-bull rampant.
47. A demi-wolf rampant.
48. An oxen head and neck couped.
49. A talbot's head and neck gorged contournee.
50. A camel statant.
51. Issuant from a diadem, a bull's head and neck.
52. A bull courant.
53. A bull's head and neck couped, holding in its mouth a Fleur de Lys fessways.
54. A bull's head and neck erased, gorged, holding in its mouth a biparted lance fessways.
55. A talbot's head and neck couped.
56. A bull's head and neck erased, gorged with a diadem.
57. Issuant from a diadem, a demi-bull accule.
58. A long horned steer's head caboshed.
59. Issuant from a diadem, a demi-bull accule.

Fig.
1. A stag statant.
2. A stag's head and neck erased arrete.
3. Issuant from a diadem, a stag's head and neck gorged with a diadem.
4. A demi-stag accule, enfiled from back to front by an arrow.
5. A stag's head and neck erased.
6. A demi-stag accule, holding an anchor erect.
7. Issuant from a ducal crown, a doe's head and neck arrete.
8. A goat's head and neck couped; in its mouth a branch of laurel sprigged and leaved; the neck charged with mullets 1, 2, and 1.
9. On a mount, a stag trippant.
10. A wolf sejant.
11. A doe's head and neck couped, gorged with a diadem and chained.
12. A goat's head couped atop two horns crossed.
13. On a mount, a doe lodged.
14. A stag's head caboshed.
15. A stag lodged.
16. A stag passant, surmounting a tree accrued.
17. A stag's head and neck couped.
18. A demi-goat accule, gorged with a diadem.
19. A goat's head and neck erased.
20. Issuant from a diadem, a ram's head and neck.
21. A goat's head and neck erased, gorged; the collar charged with three crescents.

Fig.
22. Issuant from a crown, a goat's head and neck.
23. A ram's head caboshed.
24. A goat's head and neck erased, bezantee. *See roundels in dictionary.*
25. A stag's head and neck couped arrete, surmounting two battleaxes in pile.
26. A goat's head and neck erased, collared vair and chained; surmounted at the base by an escallop between two pheons.
27. A goat's head and neck couped.
29. A stag's head caboshed.
30. A stag statant at gaze.
31. A goat passant, in its mouth a sprig of oak slipped, leaved, and fructed.
32. A ram's head caboshed.
33. A goat statant.
34. A lamb passant.
35. A goat statant.
36. A goat accule, gorged.
37. A ram passant.
38. A Paschal Lamb carrying a banner charged with the cross of St. George.
39. A ram's head and neck erased.
40. A Paschal Lamb carrying a staff and pennon charged with a cross.
41. A ram's head and neck couped, gorged, holding an olive branch in its mouth.
42. A goat statant, gorged with a diadem, and chained.
43. A lamb lodged.

Fig.
1. Issuant from a diadem, a dragon's head gorged.
2. Issuant from an embattled tower, a demi-dragon rampant; its dexter claw holding a pennant flying.
3. A wivern.
4. A demi-wolf rampant.
5. A wivern.
6. A wolf's head and neck couped, enfiled through the neck from back to front by a sword biparted.
7. A griffin rampant.
8. A dragon's head and neck couped.
9. Atop a mural crown, a dragon's head and neck erased, gorged with a diadem and chained.
10. A legless wivern or serpent dragon.
11. A wolf's head and neck couped, enfiled through the neck from back to front by a sword biparted.
12. A griffin's head erased; in its beak a pair of dividers — the neck charged with seven crescents bend sinisterways, 1, 2, 2, and 2.
13. A griffin's head, neck, and wings couped.
14. A griffin's head and neck erased, gorged.
15. Issuant from a crown, a griffin's head and neck between two wings erect.
16. A dragon's head erased and gorged.
17. Atop a chapeau, a lion, with a dragon's head and neck, couchant.
18. A demi-dragon rampant, with its dexter claw clutching an arrow point downward.
19. On a laurel branch fessways, a griffin's head, neck, and wings couped.
20. A dragon's head and neck erased; in its mouth a dexter hand apaumy.

Fig.
21. A griffin's head and neck erased, gorged with a diadem.
22. A griffin's head and neck erased, ducally gorged.
23. Atop a chapeau, a wivern.
24. A griffin's head and neck erased, gorged.
25. On a laurel branch fessways, a griffin's head, neck, and wings couped.
26. A dragon's head and neck erased; in its mouth a sinister hand apaumy.
27. Issuant from a diadem, a dragon's head gorged.
28. A dragon passant.
29. A griffin passant.
30. A demi-griffin rampant, its dexter claw holding a mullet.
31. A dragon passant.
32. A demi-wolf rampant.
33. A dragon's head and neck couped, between two wings erect.
34. A griffin statant.
35. A dragon's head and neck erased; the neck enfiled from front to back by a broken lance in bend sinister — the mouth pierced by the rest of the lance in pale, point upwards.
36. On a mount, a dragon passant.
37. A wolf's head and neck erased.
38. A dragon's head and neck erased.
39. Atop a fallen log accrued afresh, a wivern.
40. A dragon's head and neck erased; in its mouth a dexter hand apaumy.
41. A demi-wolf rampant.
42. A wivern.

49

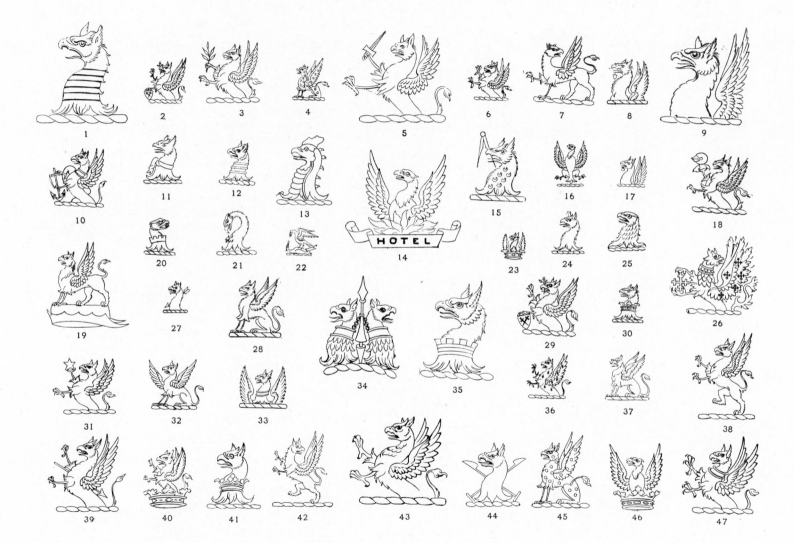

1

2

3

4

5

6

7

8

9

10

11

12

13

14

HOTEL

15

16

17

18

19

20

21

22

23

24

25

26

27

28

29

30

31

32

33

34

35

36

37

38

39

40

41

42

43

44

45

46

47

Fig.

1. A demi-eagle rampant, wings elevated; its dexter claw clutching an olive branch.

2. Issuant from a diadem, a griffin's head and neck gorged, between two wings erect.

3. An eagle in her piety.

4. An eagle's head and neck erased, a sprig of laurel in its beak.

5. On a mount, an eagle gorged and chained, with its dexter claw on a serpent nowed; its sinister wing charged with three crescents.

6. A demi-eagle displayed.

7. Issuant from a diadem, a demi-eagle displayed.

8. On a chapeau, an eagle with its wings disclosed.

9. An eagle's head issuant from flames.

10. A serpent nowed, being attacked by an eagle.

11. An eagle rising, its breast surmounted by a shield charged with a serpent nowed.

12. A bicapitated eagle displayed, surmounted by a shield charged with a lion passant; in the eagle's dexter claw a royal sceptre bendways, in its sinister claw a mond — the whole ensigned by a Sovereign Crown.

13. A bicapitated eagle displayed.

14. A cock lying on its back, being attacked by an eagle close.

15. A griffin's head and neck erased; in its beak a serpent with its tail nowed.

16. A wivern.

17. An eagle displayed, each claw clutching a signet letter; each wing charged with a pallet.

18. An eagle reguardant, its wings disclosed.

19. Issuant from flames, a demi-eagle displayed; its beak clutching a lance erect which surmounts the chest and flames — each wing charged with two links of a chain in pale.

20. An eagle displayed, with its claws resting on the torse; holding a rose in its beak paleways.

21. A demi-eagle wings segreant, with a mascle in its beak.

Fig.

22. An eagle with its wings disclosed.

23. An eagle displayed with wings disclosed, in each claw a Latin Cross.

24. Issuant from a diadem, a demi-eagle displayed bicapitated; surmounted by a shield charged with a man's head couped at the shoulders.

25. On a chapeau turned up ermine, an eagle's head and neck erased; the neck charged with a fetterlock.

26. A falcon with wings disclosed.

27. On a mount a falcon with wings disclosed, gorged with a diadem.

28. An eagle displayed.

29. An eagle in her piety.

30. A griffin passant.

31. A bicapitated eagle displayed.

32. A griffin's head and neck erased.

33. An eagle's head and neck erased.

34. An eagle's head and neck erased, gorged; atop the winged Cap of Hermes.

35. An eagle with wings displayed, its dexter claw raised holding a spear bendways.

36. A griffin's head and neck erased, gorged; clutching in its beak a branch with two roses — the neck surmounted below the collar by a shield charged with a martlet close.

37. An eagle's head and neck erased, gorged, holding in its beak a pheon point downward.

38. An eagle displayed, each claw clutching a signet letter; each wing charged with a pallet.

39. An eagle's head and neck erased, the neck enfiled by a sword bendways point downward.

40. Issuant from a mural crown, a falcon's head and neck between two wings erect.

41. An eagle displayed.

42. A griffin's head and neck between two wings erect, surmounted at the bottom by three roses barbed.

53

Fig.
1. An eagle rising.
2. A swan naiant, wings elevated.
3. A swan vorant a fish.
4. An eagle in her piety. *See piety in dictionary.*
5. An eagle in her piety, wings elevated.
6. A falcon with wings displayed, gorged, its dexter claw resting on a shield charged with a Latin Cross.
7. An eagle vulning.
8. A falcon rising.
9. A swan with wings elevated.
10. Issuant from a diadem, a demi-ostrich displayed.
11. On a mount inclaved, an ostrich close.
12. A swan close.
13. A swan's head erased, holding in its beak a key bendways.
14. A pelican vulning, its dexter claw on a rose.
15. A Cornish Chough with wings elevated; its dexter claw supporting a lance, point to chief paleways.
16. A dove close, with an olive branch in its beak.
17. A Cornish Chough close.
18. A swan rising.
19. A goose contournee.
20. An ostrich close, with a horseshoe in its beak.
21. A dove-hawk close.

Fig.
22. A Cornish Chough close.
23. A pelican vulning; its dexter claw on a rose.
24. A falcon close, gorged.
25. A swan naiant among bulrushes.
26. A dolphin on its back ensigned by a Cornish Chough.
27. On a mount, a dove encircled by a serpent.
28. On a Cap of Hermes, an eagle's head erased.
29. On a stump accrued, a Cornish Chough close.
30. A hawk rising.
31. A sparrow close, with a fish in its beak.
32. A dove close contournee, its sinister claw on a rose stem slipped and fructed.
33. A peacock close, its dexter claw on a rose.
34. A falcon close.
35. On a stump accrued, a Cornish Chough close.
36. A falcon close on a perch.
37. Between two branches raguly; a falcon with its wings disclosed, the under side of each wing charged with a mullet.
38. Under a laurel branch nowed, a dove close.
39. A falcon with wings displayed, its dexter claw on a shield charged with a Fleur de Lys.
40. A dove perched on the ring of a lantern.
41. A Cornish Chough surmounting a bulrush; its dexter claw on a Fleur de Lys bendways.

55

Fig.

1. A demi-eagle displayed, barbed and crested.
2. A falcon with wings disclosed.
3. Atop a tower embattled, a serpent being attacked by an eagle.
4. A cock close.
5. A Cornish Chough close, atop a chapeau turned up ermine.
6. On a mount, a cornucopia fessways, upon which is standing a stork close.
7. A falcon close.
8. A peacock in its pride.
9. A rowelled spur erect between two wings erect.
10. Issuant from a diadem, a demi-ostrich displayed.
11. A falcon close with a trefoile in its beak; in its dexter claw a cross pattee fitched.
12. A bee displayed en Arriere.
13. A falcon with its wings disclosed.
14. A dolphin on its back ensigned by a Cornish Chough.
15. An eagle's head erased.
16. A crane with its wings elevated, holding a sprig of laurel in its beak.
17. Three annulets interlaced; thereon a dove with an olive branch in its beak, and charged on its neck with a chevron.
18. On a mural crown; a cock close, with an olive branch in its beak, its dexter claw on a lozenge.
19. A cock with its wings displayed.
20. On a column, a dove with an olive branch in its beak, its wings displayed.
21. Issuant from a diadem, five ostrich feathers panache; ensigned by a falcon with its wings disclosed.
22. A stork close.
23. A martlet volant.
24. A dove with its wings disclosed, and an olive branch in its beak.
25. On a mount, a stork gorged, close; its dexter claw raised holding a saltire.
26. An owl close ducally crowned.
27. A swan's head and neck erased.
28. A Coat of Arms.

Fig.

29. A Cornish Chough, its dexter claw raised, holding a Caduceus bendways.
30. A falcon close.
31. A wivern, its wings segreant.
32. A woman close girt, couped at the knees, holding a pair of scales in her dexter hand.
33. A demi-man unvested; his dexter hand holding a fireball, in his sinister hand a scroll.
34. A demi-man girted with a wreath of laurel; his dexter arm embowed, the hand holding a battleaxe bend sinisterways.
35. A maiden's head couped at the shoulders.
36. A Moor's head couped at the shoulders.
37. A Moor's head couped at the shoulders.
38. A maiden close girt couped at the knees, hands together over her bosom; in the dexter hand a sickle bendways, and in the sinister hand a staff of wheat bend sinisterways.
39. A maiden close girt couped at the knees, with arms displayed; in her dexter hand a laurel wreath in orle, and in her sinister hand a rose slipped and leaved.
40. A mermaid combing her hair with her sinister hand; her dexter hand holding a mirror in pale.
41. A man's head bearded, couped at the shoulders, crowned with a diadem.
42. A Moor's head couped at the shoulders.
43. Issuant from a ducal crown, a Moor's head couped at the shoulders.
44. A man unvested, holding before him an eradicated tree bendways.
45. A bearded man couped at the waist, surmounted by a strip of laurel fessways, his dexter hand against his chest holding a club bendways.
46. Three Moors' heads co-joined of a single neck couped.
47. A bearded demi-man unvested, his dexter hand holding a battleaxe over his shoulder bend sinisterways.
48. A Moor's head couped at the shoulders.
49. A Moor's head couped, surmounted by two eight pointed mullets in fess.

1

2 3 4 5 6 7 8 9

10 11 12 13 21 14 15 16 17

26 18 19 20 22 23 24 25

27 28 29 30 31 32 33

34 35 36 37 38 39 40 41 42

MORTON

43 44 45 46 47 48 49 50

58

Fig.
1. A horse's head and neck erased.
2. A horse's head and neck erased, enfiled through the neck bendways by a spear point downward.
3. A demi-horse accule.
4. A unicorn's head erased, charged on the neck with five six pointed mullets 1, 2, and 2.
5. A unicorn's head and neck erased, gorged with a diadem.
6. A unicorn's head and neck couped, between two, and surmounted by one, Fleur de Lys.
7. A goat statant, gorged and chained.
8. Issuant from a mural crown, a horse's head and neck gorged with a diadem.
9. A horse's head and neck erased.
10. A demi-unicorn accule and collared.
11. A horse passant.
12. A demi-unicorn accule and collared.
13. A sea horse couchant.
14. A unicorn passant.
15. On a ducal crown, a horse passant, saddled and bridled.
16. A demi-pegasus accule, wings segreant.
17. A demi-horse accule, bridled; a Sovereign Crown resting on its sinister foreleg.
18. A unicorn passant reguardant.
19. Issuant from a mural crown, a horse's head and neck gorged with a diadem.
20. Issuant from a ducal crown, a unicorn's head and neck.
21. On a ducal crown, a horse passant, saddled and bridled.
22. Issuant from a ducal crown, a unicorn's head and neck.
23. A horse's head and neck couped.
24. Issuant from an embattled crown, a unicorn's head and neck.
25. A horse accule.

Fig.
26. A unicorn's head and neck erased, charged with a chevron vair.
27. A horse bridled and reined, bezantee.
28. A unicorn passant reguardant.
29. A sea horse couchant, between its forelegs a roundel.
30. A horse courant, bezantee.
31. A sea horse couchant, between its forelegs a roundel.
32. A horse statant bridled.
33. A demi-horse accule, enfiled through the shoulder by an arrow.
34. A dolphin embowed guardant, naiant in a sea undy, surmounting two tridents in pile.
35. A squirrel sejant erect, eating an acorn.
36. An owl close guardant, crowned with a diadem.
37. A dolphin embowed.
38. A spear in pale rising from the water, enfilated by a dolphin embowed.
39. A dolphin embowed.
40. A squirrel sejant erect, eating leaves.
41. A squirrel sejant erect, eating leaves.
42. A dolphin embowed, guardant, contournee.
43. A cock's head and neck erased, between two wings erect.
44. A squirrel sejant erect, holding in its sinister paw a rose slipped, leaved, and fructed; all between two escallops.
45. On a stump accrued afresh, a squirrel sejant erect, eating a berry.
46. A squirrel sejant erect, holding in its sinister paw a rose slipped, leaved, and fructed; all between two escallops.
47. A cock close.
48. A cock close.
49. A quail close among bulrushes.
50. A cock close, gorged and chained.

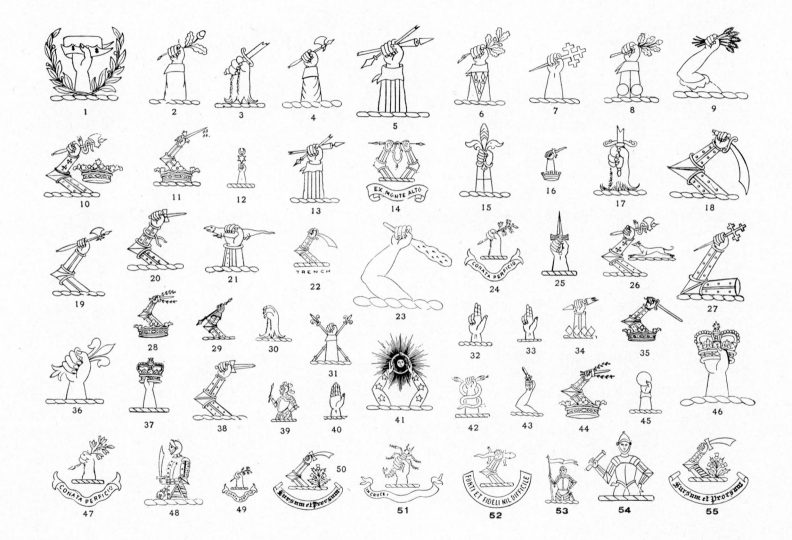

Fig.

1. A dexter cubit arm holding a chapeau turned up ermine between two laurel branches co-joined in orle.
2. A dexter cubit arm, vested and cuffed, holding a sprig of oak slipped and fructed.
3. A dexter gamb erased, holding a broken sword bend sinisterways.
4. A dexter cubit arm vested, holding a Lochober Axe bend sinisterways.
5. A dexter cubit arm, vested and cuffed, holding two parts of a broken lance.
6. A dexter cubit arm, vested and cuffed, holding a sprig of oak slipped and fructed.
7. A dexter cubit arm holding a cross crosslet fitchee bend sinisterways.
8. Behind two roundels fessways, a dexter cubit arm vested and cuffed, holding a sprig of oak slipped and fructed.
9. A dexter arm embowed, couped at the shoulder, vested to the elbow, holding five stalks of wheat fessways.
10. A dexter arm vambraced embowed, couped at the shoulder, charged on the forearm with two cross crosslets; the hand holding a battle-axe upon which a serpent is entwined, all to the dexter side of a ducal crown.
11. Issuant from a diadem, a dexter arm vambraced embowed, holding a sword embrued bend sinisterways.
12. A dexter cubit arm, fist clenched, beneath a six pointed mullet which is ensigned by a crescent.
13. A dexter cubit arm, vested and cuffed, holding two parts of a broken lance.
14. Two arms vambraced embowed, couped at the shoulder, holding a lance in fess, from which is suspended a spur.
15. A dexter cubit arm, the forearm quartered, holding a Fleur de Lys, the upper pale of which is charged with two chevronels.

Fig.

16. Issuant from an embattled crown, a dexter cubit arm holding a dirk, the blade wavy, in bend sinisterways.
17. A dexter gamb erased, holding a broken sword erect.
18. A dexter arm vambraced embowed, couped at the shoulder, holding a scimitre bendways point downward.
19. A dexter arm vambraced embowed, couped at the shoulder, holding a battleaxe bend sinisterways.
20. A dexter arm vambraced embowed, couped at the shoulder, holding a daggar fessways.
21. A dexter cubit arm vambraced, holding an alligator fessways.
22. A dexter arm vambraced embowed, couped at the shoulder, holding a scimitre bendways point downward.
23. A dexter arm embowed, couped at the shoulder, holding a spiked club bendways.
24. A dexter gamb couped, holding a sprig of laurel slipped and fructed bend sinisterways.
25. A dexter cubit arm holding a daggar erect.
26. A dexter arm vambraced embowed, couped at the shoulder, charged on the forearm with two cross crosslets; the hand holding a battleaxe upon which a serpent is entwined, all to the dexter side of a greyhound courant.
27. A dexter arm embowed acute, vambraced, couped at the shoulder, the upper arm lying fessways on the torse; the hand holding a cross crosslet fitchee bend sinisterways.
28. Issuant from the sinister side of a diadem, a dexter arm vambraced embowed, holding a sword fessways, the blade of which is between two laurel branches disposed in orle.
29. A dexter arm vambraced embowed, couped at the shoulder; the hand vested in a gauntlet, holding a lance bend sinisterways point downward.

30. A sinister gamb erased.
31. A dexter cubit arm, vested and cuffed; the hand clenched, surmounting two sceptres Fleury in saltire.
32. A dexter hand couped at the wrist, the thumb and first two fingers erect.
33. A dexter hand couped at the wrist, the thumb and first two fingers erect.
34. A dexter cubit arm vambraced, holding the butt of a broken lance bend sinisterways, all behind four lozenges fessways.
35. Issuant from a diadem, a dexter arm vambraced embowed, holding a sword bendways point downward.
36. A dexter cubit hand holding a Fleur de Lys bend sinisterways.
37. A sinister cubit arm holding a Sovereign Crown.
38. A dexter arm vambraced embowed, couped at the shoulder, holding a daggar fessways.
39. A demi-knight vambraced, his dexter arm embowed; the hand holding a broken lance erect.
40. A dexter hand couped at the wrist, erect apaumy.
41. Two arms embowed, couped at the shoulder, disposed in orle, both vested and each charged with three mullets; the hands holding a serpent, forming a circle with the tail in its mouth, all surmounting a moon in her detriment.
42. A dexter cubit arm grasping two serpents which are entwined about the forearm.
43. A dexter arm embowed, couped at the shoulder, holding a pistol.

44. Issuant from the sinister side of a diadem, a dexter arm vambraced embowed, holding a sword fessways, the blade of which is between two laurel branches disposed in orle.
45. A dexter cubit arm, vested and cuffed, holding a mullet.
46. A dexter cubit arm, holding a Sovereign Crown.
47. A dexter gamb couped, holding a sprig of laurel slipped and fructed bend sinisterways.
48. A demi-knight in profile, his sinister arm embowed, holding a scimitre erect.
49. A dexter gamb couped, holding a sprig of laurel slipped and fructed bend sinisterways.
50. A dexter arm vambraced embowed, couped at the shoulder, holding a scimitre fessways, all to the dexter side of a bush of thistle fructed, leaved, and accrued.
51. A dexter hand, couped at the wrist, grasping a scorpion bend sinisterways.
52. A dexter arm vambraced embowed, couped at the shoulder, holding an alligator displayed fessways.
53. A demi-knight, his dexter hand supporting a spear paleways, its pennon flying; his sinister arm embowed, the hand resting on the hilt of a sword.
54. A demi-knight battonnee.
55. A dexter arm vambraced embowed, couped at the shoulder, holding a scimitre fessways, all to the dexter side of a bush of thistle fructed, leaved, and accrued.

6

JE VOLL DROIT AVOIR

7

SPES·BONA

8

FOR·BEAR

Spofford

RATHER DEATHE THAN FALSE OF FAYTHE

9

10

Baron Donington

TENEBRAS MEAS

11

2

3

4

MANENT OPTIMA CŒLO   SIC VIRESCO

SPES · TUTISSIMA · CŒLIS

CONCORDIA CRESCIMUS

COPIOSE ET OPPORTUNE

5

6

7

1

2

3

4

5

FLORAT QUI LABORAT

1

SIT DEUS IN STUDIIS

2

WIN·DOR·CA·LE

WIMBLEDON SURRY S.W.

CREDE CRUCI

HONESTA·QUAM·MAGNA

4

VERITAS NON QUÆRIT ANGULOS

3

INTEGRITAS IN PROPOSITO

7

HERIOT OF RAMORNIE. 8

TRUE AND TRUSTY

NEWARK CASTLE

PAX ET COPIA

REBUS NON VERBIS

Dum recius sequeris

9

1 — I HOPE TO SHARE — RIDDELL — *Francis Asbury Riddle*

2 — VARIÆ · SUNT · FORTUNÆ · VICES — James B. Latimer.

3 — STEADFAST — William Rose Mansfield. Baron Sandhurst.

4 — SPERO MELIORA — *Alexr. Laurie Dewar.*

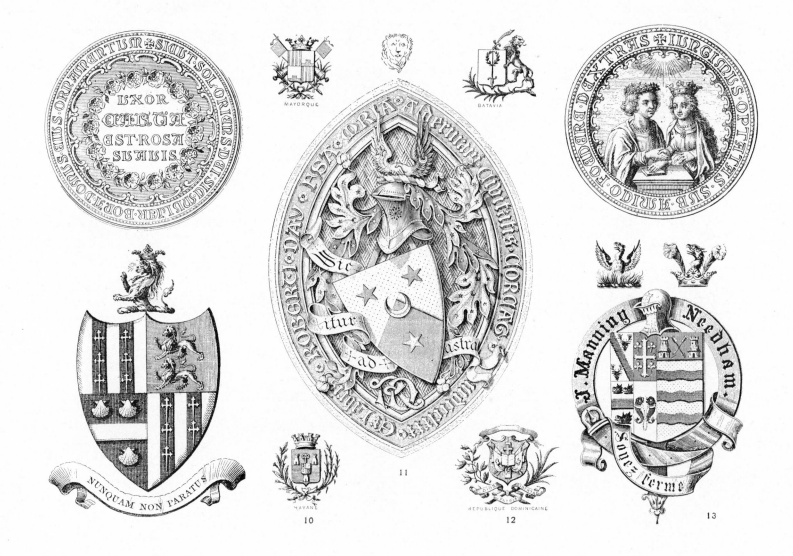

UXOR
CASTA
EST·ROSA
SUAUIS

MAYORQUE

BATAVIA

NUNQUAM NON PARATUS

HAVANE

10

11

REPUBLIQUE DOMINICAINE

12

J. Manning   Needham.

Sonez ferme

13

BELGIEN

ITALY

GRÈCI

BRAZIL

MOLLAND

AUSTRIA

NOUVELLE GRENADE

COLOMBIE

GUATEMALA

RUSSIA

NICARAGUA

PORTUGAL

SWEDEN

TURKEY

DANEMARK

SPAIN

69

CONFÉDÉRATION ARGENTINE

CHILI

MEXICO

HONDURAS

ROYAUME DE SIAM

GREAT BRITTAIN

FRANCE ROYALE

JAPAN

MOROCCO

HUNGARY

TUNIS

EGYPT

1 SAVOY HOTEL

2 HATCHETT'S

3 MARIA V. DE LUGO

4 NEC CEDE MALIS

5 HYDE PARK HOTEL

6 MOSELEY CRICKET CLUB

7 PICCADILLY HOTEL

8 SEMPER EADEM

9 FIFE ARMS HOTEL

10 AKTAION

11 HONI SOIT QUI MAL Y PENSE

12 St. ENOCH STATION HOTEL

13 CAVALRY CLUB

14 GROSVENOR HOTEL LONDON

15 EAST MIDDLESEX 77 THE DUKE OF CAMBRIDGE'S OWN

16 METROPOLE CANNES

17

18 FIRST AVENUE HOTEL

19 HOTEL METROPOLE FOLKESTONE

HYDE PARK HOTEL

1

MITCHELLS & BUTLERS LTD
WHITE HORSE HOTEL

2

DE VERE HOTEL

3

MIDLAND HOTEL
BIRMINGHAM

4

BOOTH
QUOD ERO SPERO

5

TRADE MARK

6

TOYO KISEN KAISHA

7

CANADIAN PACIFIC RAILWAY

8

SPECTEMUR AGENDO
EGYPT
BADAJOZ XXX SEVASTOPOL
SALAMANCA INKERMAN
PENINSULA WATERLOO ALMA
CHITRAL

9

10

B.C.H.Co.Ld.

11

PRISCA FIDES

12

CONSERVATIVE CLUB

13

PER AC
AR LTA
DUA 圆

14

GLORIA IN EXCELSIS DEO

15

BIRMINGHAM RESTAURANT
G.W.R.

16

WHITE HART HOTEL

17

COMPAÑIA BARCELONA
TRASATLANTICA

18

FORTITUDE ET FIDELITAS
DUMBARTONSHIRE VOLUNTEERS

19

CAVALRY CLUB

15

16

17

18

PROPTER LIBERTATEM

SAVOY HOTEL

19

VICTORIA STEAMBOAT ASSOCIATION LTD

V

22

L&N.W.R.C°

St ERMIN'S HOTEL

WESTMINSTER

24

23

HONI·SOIT·QUI·MAL·Y·PENSE

20

21

25

AMERICAN LINE

26

HOLDER

NISI DOMINUS FRUSTRA

29

CLIFTONVILLE HOTEL

30

QUE SUO CRESCIT INCITAIRE PERIT

31

UNITED SERVICE CLUB

32

REFORM CLUB

33

ULSTER CLUB

27

HONI·SOIT·QUI·MAL·Y·PENSE

28

35

ROW THUS

37

HONI SOIT QUI MAL Y PENSE

DIEU ET MON DROIT

36

34

38

MODERN GERMAN GOTHIC

ABCDEFGHIKM
NOPQRSTUVW
abcde XYZ fghikl
mnoprsqtuvwxyz

FRENCH CURSIV

ABCDEFGHH
IJKLMNOPQ
RSTTUVWXY

MODERN FRENCH

ABCDEFGHIJKL
MNOPQRSTUW
VXYZ
123456789 &

CHURCH TEXT

ABCDEFGH
IJKLMNOP
QRSTUVW
XYZ

OLD ENGLISH

A few of the most
useful and
Pleasing Alphabets
seen in
Heraldic
and other
Art Designs.
Etc.

GERMAN GOTHIC

ABCDEFGHI
KLMNOPQR
STUVWXY
abcdefghiklm
nopqrstuvw
xyz

GERMAN UNCIALS

ABCDEFGHI
JKLMNOPQR
STUVWXYZ
GERMAN 14th Cent.

FRENCH SCRIPT

ABCDEFGHI
JKLMNOPQS
RTTUVWXY

MODERN ROMAN

ABCDEFGHIJKLM
NOPQRSTUVW
abcdef XYZ ghijklm
nopqrstuvxwzy MB

METHOD

O AND Q

EXERCISE FOR PEN AND GRAVER.

Grace L. Howard
OLD ENGLISH

Alice W. Newcomb

SHADED OLD ENGLISH

SHADED PEARL ROMAN

Isa F. Stephon
SHADED OLD-ENG

From ART MONOGRAMS AND LETTERING *by* J. M. Bergling
Copyright by V. C. Bergling

76

Dictionary of Heraldic Terms

ABAISSE — ABASED: Any ordinary which is at or above the fess point or center point, is *abaisse* when placed in the lower part of the shield. *See Page 25, Figure 4.*

ABATEMENT — ABATEMENT OF HONOUR: A figure added to the arms to denote illegitimacy. *See baton sinister and bordure compony.*

ABLAZE: Blazing, having flames.

ACCOUTRED: Vested, dressed.

ACCRUED: Growing.

ACCRUED AFRESH: Applied to a stump or a fallen log which is sprouting. *Page 35, Figure 15.*

ACCULE: A position similar to rampant, but with the hoofs or paws pointed downward. *Page 27, Figures 19 and 53, also Page 42, Figure 57.*

ACHIEVEMENT — HATCHMENT: A full coat of arms.

ADDORSED — ADDORSEE: Placed back to back. *Page 27, Figure 18 and Page 50, Figure 34.*

ADUMBRATED — DETRIMENT: Overshadowed, eclipsed. A moon in eclipse is termed *in her detriment* or *adumbrated. Page 60, Figure 41.*

AFFRONTED — AFFRONTEE: Face to face, or facing the observer. *Page 27, Figure 24.*

AFIRE: *See ablaze.*

AJOURE: *Page 23, Figure 38.*

ALLERION: An eagle displayed without beak or claws. *Page 27, Figure 42.*

ALTERNATELY: Roses and roundels alternately would mean a rose, a roundel, a rose, a roundel, etc.

AMBULANT: Walking. *Page 27, Figure 21, and Page 34, Figure 9.*

ANNULET: A charge in the form of a circle. It is also a mark of cadency or difference for the fifth son. *See Page 19, Cadency and Page 25, Figure 33.*

ANCIENT: As a noun, this means a flag or its bearer; as an adjective it means very old, obsolete.

ANGLED: A form of a line. *See Page 19, lines.*

ANSERATED: Charged with a goose. *See Page 21, Figure 9.*

APALMY — APAUMY: An open hand with the palm facing the observer. *See Page 25, Figure 44, and Page 35, Figure 19.*

ARCHED: A form of a line. *See double arched. Also Page 23, Figures 18 and 22.*

ARGENT: Silver. One of the two metals used in Heraldry.

ARMED: When parts of a figure are of a different tincture from that of the body, this condition is described by making a verb of that particular part, and following the verb with the colour or metal; for example, *a falcon black, armed gold. Armed* refers to those parts of a figure used for fighting, such as claws, beaks, horns, fangs, tusks, etc.

ARMS OF AUGMENTATION: Marks of honour granted by the Sovereign. They are placed on the family arms in quarter, chief, or canton. *See Page 25, Figures 22 and 24, Page 34, Figure 7, Chaney.*

ARMS PARLANTES — CANTING ARMS — PUNNING ARMS: Arms taken from the name of the bearer; for example, the heart and fetterlock in the arms of Lockhart; a hawk on a perch for Hawker; three arrows for Archer; three herring for Herringham, etc.

ARRETE — AT GAZE: A position of the head the same as guardant, but the gaze is supposed to be more intent. This term is used with reference to the deer family. *See page 27, Figure 29, and Page 44, Figure 2.*

ARRIERE — EN ARRIERE: A figure with its back to the observer. *See Page 56, Figure 12.*

ASPECTANT: Animals face to face, not *combatant.*

ASPERSED — ASPERSEE — SEMEE: Powdered, strewed, sprinkled with. *See Page 25, Figure 5.*

ASSISE — SEJANT: Sitting on the hind legs; applied to four legged animals. *See Page 27, Figure 10.*

ASSUMPTIVE: Arms used without proper authority.

ASSURGANT: A figure rising from water. *See Page 27, Figure 45.*

AT GAZE: *See arrete. Also Page 44, Figure 7.*

ATTIRED: Same as *armed*, but applied to antlers.

AUGMENT: A verb; the act of applying an augmentation.

AUGMENTATION: *See arms of augmentation.*

AVERSANT: Turned away. *See Page 25, Figure 43.*

AXE: *See battleaxe, Lochober Axe. See Page 34, Figure 13.*

BANDEAU — TORSE — WREATH: *See Page 13, Paragraph 3.*

BANDED — BANDAGED: Tied with a band. *See Page 25, Figure 15, and Page 31, Figure 14.*

BANNER: A type of flag, usually displaying Arms.

BAR: *See fess.*

BARB: A backward projecting point on a weapon designed to make removal difficult. *See Page 25, Figure 20.*

BARBED: Having a beard; bearing leaves; when used in reference to a rose, it has the same meaning as *armed* regarding the small leaves between the petals of a rose. *See armed. See Page 25, Figures 18 and 21.*

BARBEL: A species of fish.

BARDINGS: Horse trappings bearing arms. *Barded* is sometimes used to indicate the tincture of the *bardings. See Page 31, Figure 2.*

BARS GEMEL: *See fess.*

BARRULET: *See Fess.*

BARRY: *See Fess.*

BARWAYS — BARWISE: Crossing the field horizontally. *See fess.*

BASE: Lower or bottom third of the shield.

BATTLEAXE: Military weapon. *See Page 60, Figure 10.*

BATON — BATUNE — BASTON: *See bend sinister.*

BATTONNEE: Carrying or charged with a baton. *See Page 27, Figure 13.*

BEAKED: The same as *armed*, but pertaining only to the beak.

BEARDED: *See barbed.*

BEAVER: That part of a helmet which protects the eyes and can be raised. *See Page 39, Figure 4.*

BELLED: Charged with bells. *See Page 28, Figure 13.*

BEND: An honourable ordinary drawn on the shield from the dexter chief to the sinister base. If charged, its size is one-third the shield; if uncharged, one-fifth the shield. *See Page 17, Bottom Figure 2.* This term is compounded to denote position or direction *in bend* or *bendways, see Page 35, Figure 14,* and partition *per bend, see Page 21, Figure 10.* The bend has three dimunitives:

BENDLET: One-half the width of a bend. *See Page 17, Bottom 9.*

COTISE: One-fourth the width of a bend; one-half the width of a bendlet.

RIBAND: Two-thirds the width of a bendlet; one-sixth the width of a shield.

The cotises are frequently disposed on each side of a bend, and usually of a different tincture from the bend they border. This is similar to *fimbriated,* but applying only to bends.

BENDY: Divided by several bends of alternate metal and colour.

BEND SINISTER: A reverse bend drawn from sinister chief to dexter base; not an honourable ordinary, but an *abatement.* This term is compounded to denote position or direction *in bend sinister* or *bend sinisterways, see Page* 34, *Figure* 13, and partition *per bend sinister, see Page* 21, *Figure* 14. The bend sinister has two dimunitives:

SCRAPE: One-half the width of the bend sinister.

BATON — BATUNE — BASTON: One-half the width of a *scrape;* one-fourth the width of a bend sinister and couped at the ends. *See Page* 15, *last Paragraph.*

BATTONNEE: Bearing, *see Page* 27, *Figure* 13, or charged with a baton.

BESANT — BEZANT — BYZANT: A gold roundel. *See roundels.*

BESANTED — BESANTEE: Semee of *besants. See Page* 42, *Figure* 12.

BEVELLED — BEVELLY: Form of a line. *See Page* 19, *lines.*

BICAPITATED: Two-headed. *See Page* 27, *Figure* 14.

BICORPORATED: Two figures with a common head. *See Page* 27, *Figure* 15.

BILLET: A charge of oblong shape, such as a brick or billet. *See Page* 25, *Figure* 7.

BILLETTY: Semee of billets. *See Page* 25, *Figure* 7.

BIPARTED: Broken into two pieces, with both pieces shown. *See Page* 27, *Figure* 39.

BLADED: Same as *armed,* but referring to the blade or wide part of a stalk of grain.

BLAZON: To describe arms in Heraldic terms.

BLAZING: Burning, afire. *See Page* 25, *Figure* 19.

BORDURE: An honourable ordinary; a border of the shield. This is a mark of difference or cadency. *See Page* 30, *Figures* 3, 5 *and* 7. There are two dimunitives of a bordure:

ORLE: An open or perforated inescutcheon; one-half a bordure. *See Page* 25, *Figure* 6.

TRESSURE: One-half an *orle,* frequently disposed double. *See Page* 25, *Figure* 31.

DOUBLE TRESSURE: *See Page* 25, *Figure* 1.

IN ORLE: Disposed in the shape of the bottom and sides of an *orle. See Page* 25, *Figure* 26.

BORDURE COMPONY: A bordure made of a single line of squares of alternate metal and colour or fur. The *bordure compony* is an abatement for illegitimacy in Scotland.

BOTTONNY: *See cross bottonny Page* 73, *Figure* 12.

BOUGET: An ancient water-bucket.

BRACED — BRASED — BRAZED: Two or more like figures interlaced. *See Page* 25, *Figure* 10.

BRANCHED: Same as *armed,* but referring to the branches of a tree or bush.

BRISSURE: A general term for marks of difference, and marks of cadency.

BROAD ARROW: An ancient missile. *See Page* 52, *Figure* 37.

BROCK: A badger. *See Page* 42, *Figure* 37.

BROUCHANT: Overlying, surmounting. *See Page* 25, *Figure* 2.

BULRUSHES: A tall plant growing in water. *See Page* 54, *Figure* 41.

CABOCHED — CABOSHED — CABOSSED: A head full faced to the observer, with no neck. *See Page* 27, *Figure* 30.

CADENCY: *See marks of cadency Page* 19.

CADUCEUS: From Mythology, the staff of Hermes, the messenger and herald of the Gods. *See Page* 56, *Figure* 29.

CALTRAP — CHEVAL TRAP: An iron instrument of four spikes cojoined so that one spike will always point upwards. They were strewn on a field to injure horses' hoofs, and thus harass mounted knights in battle. *See Page* 35, *Figure* 3.

CANTING ARMS: *See arms parlantes.*

CANTON: A small square figure placed at a corner of a shield, usually the dexter chief. *See Page 34, Figure 7, Arms of Cheney.*

CAP OF HERMES: A winged cap worn by Hermes. *See Caduceus. See Page 54, Figure 28.*

CAP OF MAINTENANCE — CHAPEAU: A cap of dignity worn by Sovereign Princes, made of crimson or scarlet velvet, lined and turned up ermine. *See Page 25, Figure 41 and Page 34, Figures 1 and 6.*

CAP OF STATE: A cap of dignity worn by higher statesmen. *See Page 25, Figure 42.*

CAT-O'-MOUNTAIN: *See Page 42, Figure 14.*

CATHERINE WHEEL: A wheel of torture tired with spikes, the type of wheel upon which St. Catherine was martyred.

CELESTIAL CROWN: A crown of longer points, with stars at the ends of the points.

CENTAUR: From Mythology — a creature made up of a man to the waist on a horse's body where the neck would usually start.

CHAMPAGNE — CHAMPAIGNE: A narrow piece cut horizontally from the base of a shield. *See Page 21, Figure 30.*

CHAPEAU: *See Cap of Maintenance.*

CHAPLET: Originally a wreath for the head; in Heraldry shown as a circular wreath used as a charge, and always in its natural colour — *proper. See Page 34, Figure 2.*

CHAPOURNET: *See Page 23, Figure 25.*

CHAPPE: *See Page 23, Figure 3.*

CHARGE: Noun — a figure placed on a field, ordinary, or sub-ordinary; verb — to place a charge on a field, ordinary, or sub-ordinary.

CHASSE: *See Page 23, Figure 31.*

CHECKY — CHEQUEY — CHEQUEE: Alternate squares of metal and colour or fur, as a checkerboard. *See Page 25, Figure 8.*

CHEQUER: A dimunitive of a *checky. See Page 25, Figure 9.*

CHEVAL TRAP: *See caltrap.*

CHEVRON: An honourable ordinary in the form of an obtuse angle, with the point or apex upward. *See Page 17, Bottom 5.* This term is used compounded to denote charges disposed in that arrangement *in chevron* and partitions of a field *per chevron. See Page 21, Figure 36.* The chevron has two dimunitives:

> CHEVRONEL: One-half the width of a *chevron. See Page 60, Figure 15.*
>
> COUPLE CLOSE: One-fourth the width of a chevron; one-half the width of a *chevronel. See Page 25, Figure 10.*

CHIEF: The upper third of a shield; also an honourable ordinary which occupies the upper third of a shield. *See Page 23 on chiefs.* This term is compounded to denote upper position *in chief.* The chief has one dimunitive:

> FILLET: One-fourth the width of a *chief,* and always placed at the botton of the *chief* (just above the fess).
>
> FILLETED: *See Page 23, Figure 8.*

CHIMERICAL FIGURES: Imaginary and mythological creatures, such as griffins, dragons, wiverns, harpies, mermaids, centaurs, etc.

CINQUE FOIL: Five leaves cojoined at the center; a mark of cadency for the ninth son; also used occasionally to term a rose. *See Page 25, Figure 36.*

CIVIC CAP: *See Cap of State.*

CIVIC CROWN: A wreath of acorns and oak leaves.

CLARION: A charge which correctly represents a lance rest, but is termed *clarion* because of its resemblance to a trumpet.

CLENCHED: The fingers or claws closed to the palm. *See Page 29, Figure 10.*

CLOSE: A position of wings; down, or close to the body. *See Page 29, Figure 11.* For other positions, see *wings.*

CLOSE GIRT: Belted around the waist. *See Page* 56, *Figures 32 and* 38.

CLOSET: *See fess.*

CLOUE: Nailed. The same as *armed,* but referring to nails or rivets.

COAT ARMOUR: A surcoat upon which armorial bearings are charged. It was worn over armour.

COCKATRICE: A chimerical creature; a cock with a wivern's tail, wings, and legs. *See Page* 50, *Figure* 13.

COJOINED: When two or more like objects are joined at the fess point or center, they are termed *cojoined. See Page* 25, *Figur*e 13.

COLLARED — GORGED: Wearing a collar.

COMBATANT: Fighting. *See Page* 27, *Figure* 17.

COMPARTMENT — MONT — MOUNT: A panel or mound at the bottom of a coat of arms, upon which the supporters, and sometimes the shield, are rested. A *mount* is often used as a rest for crests. *See Page* 38, *Figure* 13.

COMPLEMENT: A full moon is termed *in her complement. See Page* 27, *Figure* 34.

COMPLEXED: Wound together, without the use of cord. *See Page* 25, *Figure* 11.

COMPONY: *See bordure compony.*

CONCAVED: Curved inward. *See Page* 21, *Figure* 33.

CONTOURNED —CONTOURNEE —COTOURNED: Reversed, facing the sinister. *See Page* 27, *Figure* 11, *and Page* 42, *Figure* 49.

CONY: A rabbit. *See Page* 34, *Figure* 11.

CORDED: Wrapped with a cord; mostly used when the cord is of a different tincture from that of the parcel. *See armed. Also Page* 25, *Figure* 14.

CORDON: A silver cord used to encircle the arms of a widow. *See Page* 25, *Figure* 12.

CORNUCOPIA: The mythical horn of plenty. *See Page* 56, *Figure* 6.

CORONET: A crown.

CORSELET — HABERGEON — CUIRASS: Armour for the torso. *See Page* 38, *Figure* 8.

COTISE: *See bend.*

COTOURNED: *See contourned.*

COUCHANT: A position of a four legged animal lying down with its head uplifted. *See Page* 27, *Figure* 1 *and Page* 48, *Figure* 17.

COUCHEE: A term applied to shields placed in a diagonal position. *See Page* 31, *Figure* 15.

COUNTER: Opposed or contrary.

COUNTER CHANGED: When a shield, or part thereof, is divided into two parts, both of the same metal and colour, and disposed contrarywise, it is termed *counter changed. See Page* 25, *Figure* 3, *and Page* 21, *Figure* 40.

COUNTER COMPONY: A double row of alternate squares of metal and colour or fur.

COUNTER EMBATTLED: *See embattled.*

COUNTER FLEURY — COUNTER FLORY: Fleurs de Lys placed in alternate directions. *See Page* 25, *Figure* 1.

COUNTER NAIANT: Two fish swimming, one above the other, facing in opposite directions. *See Page* 27, *Figure* 25.

COUNTER PASSANT: Two animals passant, facing in opposite directions, usually one above the other. *See Page* 27, *Figure* 16.

COUNTER SALIENT: Two animals salient, facing in opposite directions, frequently disposed to form a saltire or X. *See Page* 27, *Figure* 26.

COUNTER-VAIR: Classed as a fur, represented by bells set alternately base to base. They are always blue on silver unless otherwise specified.

COUPED: Cut off in a straight line. This term is also applied to an ordinary which is cut off so that it does not reach the edges of the shield. *See Page* 19, *Figure* 4, *and Page* 21, *Figure* 1.

COUPLE CLOSE: *See chevron.*

COUR: A form of a line. *See Page* 21, *Figure* 37.

COURANT: Running. *See Page 38, Figure 2.*

COUVERT: *See Page 23, Figure 19.*

COUE — COWARD — COWARDED: A position of an animal's tail; drooping between its hind legs. *See Page 27, Figure 12, and Page 42, Figure 20.*

CRANE: *See Page 56, Figure 16.*

CRENELLE EMBATTLED: A line formed like the battlements of a wall. *See Page 19, lines.* The term *embattled* is more frequently used. When an ordinary is *embattled*, only the top or chief edge is so formed; if both edges are embattled, it is termed *counter embattled.*

CRESCENT — CRESSANT: A first quarter moon with the horns turned upward.

CREST: *See Page 12, last Paragraph.*

CRESTED: Having a comb or crest. This term applies to those figures which do not normally have a comb. When used with a cock or fowl which does normally have a comb, it indicates that the comb is of a different tincture from that of the body. *See Page 27, Figure 41 and Page 56, Figure 1.*

CRINED: Denotes hair of a different tincture from that of the body.

CROSIER: A staff ending in a crook borne by a bishop or archbishop. *See Page 32, Figure 11.*

CROSS: *See Pages 19 and 23.*

CROSS CROSSED — CROSS CROSSLET: *See Page 19, Figure 13.*

CRUSILY: Semee of *crosses crosslet.*

CUBIT ARM: A hand and arm couped at the elbow. *See Page 37, Figure 18.*

CUFFED: Having a cuff; also used when the cuff is of a different tincture from that of the sleeve. *See armed. See Page 35, Figure 8.*

CUIRASS: *See corselet.*

CURTANA: A pointless sword of mercy.

DANCETTE: A serrated line. One *dancette* is equal to three indentations. *See Page 19, lines.*

DAGGER — DIRK: A small swordlike weapon. *See Page 60, Figure 17.*

DEBRUSED: A charge surmounted by an ordinary. *See Page 66, Figure 9.*

DECRESCENT — DECRESSANT: A moon in her third quarter or wane, with the horns facing the sinister side of the shield. *See Page 27, Figure 38.*

DEGRADED: A cross with the arms ending in steps is termed *degraded. See Page 19, Figure 15.*

DEMI — DEMY: Half; example, a demi-lion. *See Page 34, Figure 12.*

DE SANG: Of blood, such as *Guttee De Sang,* meaning drops of blood.

DETRIMENT: *See adumbrated.*

DEXTER: The right side; in arms, dexter is left to the observer. *See Page 14, Paragraph 2.*

DIADEM: A crown. *See Page 37, Figure 2.*

DIBBER: A pointed tool used to make holes in the ground for planting seeds. *See Page 50, Figure 44.*

DIFFERENCE: A verb meaning to distinguish between.

DIMUNITIVE: A bearing of the same shape, but thinner or narrower.

DISCLOSED: *See wings disclosed. Page 31, Figure 15.*

DISMEMBERED: Cut in pieces, but not altered in form.

DISPLAYED: A bird whose wings and legs are spread facing the observer. *See Page 29, Figure 5.*

DISPOSED — PLACED: Self explanatory. *Disposed in orle Page 60, Figure 28; disposed in saltire, see Page 31, Figure 14.*

DOE — DEER — STAG: There are several terms for positions which apply to the deer family alone, such as *trippant, arrete, lodged,* etc., for examples, *see Page 29, Figure 3.*

DOLPHIN: *See Page* 58, *Figures* 34 *and* 37.

DORMANT: Sleeping; the posture of an animal in repose. *See Page* 27, *Figure* 3.

DOUBLINGS: The lining of robes or lambrequins.

DOUBLE ARCHED: One-half an arch. *See arched.*

DOUBLE FITCHED: *See fitched and Page* 21, *Figure* 3.

DOUBLE TRESSURE: *See bordure. Page* 25, *Figure* 1.

DOVETAILED: Form of a line. *See Page* 19, *lines.*

DRAGON: A chimerical figure with four legs. *See Page* 48, *Figures* 28 *and* 31 *for dragons, also wiverns, griffins, etc.*

DUCALLY GORGED: Gorged with a ducal or Duke's crown. *See Page* 37, *Figure* 6.

ECLIPSE. *See detriment.*

ELEVATED: A position of the wings above the head. *See Page* 56, *Figure* 16.

EMBATTLED: *See crenelle.*

EMBATTLED CROWN: A crown, the top edge of which is *embattled. See Page* 60, *Figure* 16.

EMBATTLED GRADY — GRADY — BATTLED EMBATTLED: Embattled in steps. *See Page* 21, *Figure* 35.

EMBOWED: Bent, curved, or entwined. *See Page* 34, *Figure* 13.

EMBRUED — IMBRUED: Dropping blood. *See Page* 35, *Figure* 3.

ENARCHED.

EN ARRIERE: *See arriere.*

ENDORSE: *See pale.*

ENFILED: A figure pierced through by a weapon is termed *enfiled. See Page* 42, *Figure* 23.

ENFILATED: Applies to a weapon piercing a figure. *See Page* 34, *Figure* 10.

ENGRAILED: Form of a line; bordered with small semi-circles, points turned outward. *See Page* 19, *lines.*

ENGRAVERS' TRICK: A method used by engravers to denote tincture, (metals, colours, or furs) by using arrangements of lines for colours and dots for gold, examples of which are on *Page* 17.

ENHANCED: Placed above the usual position; a *fess disposed in chief* would be *enhanced.*

ENMANCHE: *See Page* 23, *Figure* 21.

ENSIGN: Noun — a flag. *See Page* 37, *Figure* 7.

ENSIGNED: Verb — having another figure placed above. *See Page* 32, *Figure* 8.

ENTIRE: Extended to the side of the shield.

ENTWINED: Wrapped around. *See serpent entwined Page* 60, *Figure* 10.

ERADICATED: Uprooted. *See Page* 56, *Figure* 44.

ERASED: Torn off, leaving a ragged edge. *See Page* 29, *Figures* 1, 3, *and* 4.

ERECT: The verticle or *pale* position of a charge whose normal position is horizontal. *See Page* 27, *Figure* 23, *Page* 30, *Figure* 10, *Page* 34, *Figure* 10.

ERMINE: A white fur with black tufts. *See Page* 17, *tinctures, and Page* 50, *Figure* 36.

ERMINES: Ermine reversed; shown by white tufts on a sable field.

ERMINOIS: Black tufts on a field of gold.

ESCALLOP: A shell. *See Page* 35, *Figure* 17 *and Page* 40, *Figures* 28 *and* 32.

ESCARTELE: A form of a line. *See Page* 19, *lines.*

ESCROLL: Scroll. *See Page* 10, *last Paragraph.*

ESCUTCHEON: Shield. *See Page* 14, *Paragraph* 1.

ESCUTCHEON OF PRETENSE: A small escutcheon bearing the arms of a wife who is an heiress, placed surtout, or over a husband's arms, in fess point. *See Page* 25, *Figure* 23. When discussing Arms of Pretense, husband and wife are always referred to as *Baron* and *Femme*, no matter what their rank may be. This escutcheon differs from the inescutcheon, which is a small escutcheon forming a charge.

ESTOILE: An eight pointed star different from a mullet in that four points are *rayant*.

FASCES: A Roman battleaxe. *See Page* 30, *Figure* 12.

FAULCHION — SCIMITER: A sword having a curved blade.

FER de MOLINE — MILLRIND: An ancient fixture for the stone wheel of a grindstone. *See Page* 63, *Spoffard*. It is from this we get the *cross moline*, *See Page* 21, *Figure* 5.

FESS — FESSE: An honourable ordinary running horizontally across the center of the shield, and occupying one-third the area. *See ordinaries Page* 17. This word is used compounded in Heraldry to indicate a horizontal position *fessways* or *fesswise*. *See Page* 35, *Figure* 19, or a center position. *In fess* means *in center*. *See Page* 31, *Figure* 8. *Per fess* refers to partitions. *See partitions Page* 21, *Figure* 12. *Fessways* refers to anything in a horizontal position; *fess point* means center point. The fess has many dimunitives:

BAR: Occupies one-fifth of the shield. *See Page* 23, *Figure* 39.

CLOSET: Occupies one-tenth of the shield, or one-half of the *bar*. *See Page* 23, *Figures* 40 *and* 42.

BARRULET: Occupies one-twentieth of the shield, or one-fourth a *bar*, or one-half a *closet*. *See Page* 23, *Figure* 41.

BARS GEMEL: Two *bars*.

BARRE — BARRY: A series of *closets* or *barrulets* of alternate tincture, and always an even number of six or more. *See Page* 23, *Figure* 44.

BARRY WAVY: *See fountain under roundels*.

FESS POINT: The center point of the escutcheon. *See fess*.

FESSWAYS: *See fess*.

FETTERLOCK: A handcuff. *See Page* 52, *Figure* 25.

FIELD: The whole surface of the escutcheon or shield.

FIGURED: Bearings showing a human face are termed *figured*.

FILE — LABEL: A mark of cadency denoting the eldest son. *See Page* 19, *cadency*.

FILLET: *See chief*.

FIMBRIATED: An ordinary having a narrow border of a different tincture from its own. *See cotised under bends. See Page* 19, *Figure* 5.

FIREBALL: A sphere issuing flames. *See Page* 56, *Figure* 33.

FITCHEE — FITCHED — FITCHY: A term usually applied to crosses whose bottom branch is pointed so that it may be fixed into the ground. This branch is usually longer. *See Page* 19, *Figure* 17, *Page* 60, *Figure* 7. *Double fitched* — two points. *See Page* 21, *Figure* 3.

FLANCHES: *See Page* 25, *Figure* 30.

FLANK: Either side of a shield between chief and base. *See Page* 17, *Divisions of shield*.

FLASQUES: *See Page* 25, *Figure* 29.

FLEUR DE LYS: A bearing derived from the French, and was an emblem of France. It is also a mark of cadency for the sixth son. *See Page* 37, *Figure* 3, *and Page* 19, *Cadency*.

FLEURY — FLORY: Adorned with, or terminating in, Fleur de Lys. *Page* 19, *Figure* 11.

FLEAM: A surgical instrument.

FLEXED: *See embowed*.

FLORY: *See fleury. Page* 19, *Figure* 11.

FOUNTAIN: *See roundels*.

FOURCHEE: Divided into two parts.

FRANCHE — NOWY: Form of a line. *See Page* 19, *lines*.

FRET: Two laths in saltire interlaced with a mascle. *See Page* 25, *Figure* 25.

FRETTY: Covered with diagonally interlaced laths. *See Page* 32, *Figure* 4.

FRUCTED: Bearing fruit, seeds, or flowers. *See Page* 54, *Figure* 32, *and Page* 60, *Figure* 2.

FUSIL: a charge longer and narrower than a lozenge. *See Page* 25, *Figure* 40 *and Page* 35, *Figure* 11.

FUSILY: A semee of fusils. *See Page* 19, *Figure* 16.

GALLEY — LYMPHAD: A ship using both sails and oars. *See Page* 38, *Figure* 8.

GAMB: The foreleg of a beast. *See Page* 29, *Figure* 10.

GARB: A sheaf of grain. *See Page* 38, *Figure* 11.

GARNISHED: This term is used to denote the colour of the ornamentation of a charge.

GARTER — BENDLET: *See bend.*

GAUNTLET: Armour for the hand. *See Page* 60, *Figure* 29.

GAZE: *See arrete.*

GEMELS: Double. *For bars gemel see fess.*

GIRTED: Belted. *See Page* 56, *Figure* 34.

GOBONY: A compony.

GOLPS: *See roundels.*

GONFAN: A long flag attached to a crossbar on a staff.

GORE: A curved triangular piece of chain mail between plates of armour. *See Page* 21, *Figure* 38.

GORGED: Collared. *See Page* 37, *Figure* 6.

GORGES: Whirlpools.

GRADY: *See embattled grady.*

GRIFFIN — GRYPHON: A chimerical figure. *See Page* 31, *Figure* 6, *also Page* 48, *on griffins, dragons, wiverns, etc.*

GUARDANT: A position of the head; facing the observer regardless of the position of the body. *See arrete Page* 27, *Figure* 2; *see caboshed page* 34, *Figure* 1.

GUIDON: A small semi-oval flag used in funerals.

GUIGE: A belt worn over the right shoulder.

GULES: Red. *See Page* 17, *tinctures.*

GUSSET: A triangular piece of chain mail between plates of armour. *See Page* 21, *Figure* 39.

GUTTEE: Strewed semee with drops.

GUTTEE DE SANG: Semee with drops of blood.

GUZES: *See roundels.*

GYRON: A triangle, usually a right triangle, using the dexter chief point and fess point as two of the angle points, dividing the first quarter diagonally in bend. *See Page* 21, *figures* 28 *and* 29. *For round gyrones see Page* 21, *Figures* 23, 25 *and* 27.

GYRONNY: A group of gyrons covering the shield, uniting in the fess point, for a *gyronny of eight*. *See Page* 21, *Figure* 29.

HABERGEON: *See corselet.*

HABITED: Clothed, dressed. *See Page* 27, *Figure* 40.

HAME: Horse collar.

HARPY: A chimerical figure having the head and breast of a woman on the body of a bird.

HAURIANT: Position of a fish; erect, but applying only to a fish. *See Page* 27, *Figures* 23, 24 *and* 25.

HELMET: *See Page* 13, *Paragraph* 3.

HILTED: The term used when the hilt of a dagger is of a different tincture from that of the blade. *See armed.*

HIND: A female red deer.

HONOUR POINT: *See Page* 17, *divisions of the shield.*

HORNED: *See armed.*

HORSE: *See Page* 58.

HUMETTY: Applied to an ordinary that is cut off so that it does not touch the edge of the shield, but not necessarily *couped*. *See Page* 19, *Figure* 18, *crosses.*

HURT: *See roundels.*

HURST: A group of trees.

IMBRUED: Dropping blood. Do not confuse with *guttee de sang* which means a *semee* of drops of blood. *See Page* 35, *Figure* 3.

IMPALED: A term used to denote a shield parted per pale, *see Page* 32, *Figure* 16, with two coats of arms placed side by side.

INCRESCENT — INCRESSANT: A moon in her first quarter, with the horns turned toward the dexter side of the shield. *See Page* 27, *Figure* 37.

INCLAVED: *See Page* 54, *Figure* 11, *and Page* 23, *Figure* 35.

INDENTED: A serrated line used as a border. *See Page* 19, *lines.*

INESCUTCHEON: A small escutcheon used as a charge. *See Page* 39, *Figure* 2.

INVECTED: A form of a line. *See Page* 19, *lines.*

IRRADIATED: Rays of light pointing out from the center. *See Page* 37, *Figure* 14.

ISSUANT — ISSUING: Coming out of. *See Page* 27, *Figure* 7, *and Page* 37, *Figure* 16. *Also see jessant, naissant, and assurgant.*

JESSANT: Issuing from the field, or parts thereof. *See Page* 27, *Figure* 8.

JESSES: Leg straps for a hawk or falcon.

LABEL —FILE: A brissure or mark of cadency of the eldest son. *See Page* 19 *cadency.*

LAMBREQUIN — MANTLET — MANTLING: *See Page* 13, *last Paragraph.*

LANGUED: Same as *armed*, but applying only to the tongue.

LARMES: Tears.

LATIN CROSS: *See Page* 19, *crosses.*

LEAVED: Having leaves or denoting that the leaves are of a different tincture from green. *See Page* 35, *Figure* 18.

LION: *See Page* 27, *lions.*

LODGED: A position of a stag similar to *couchant*. *See Page* 31, *Figure* 13.

LOWERED: When an ordinary or sub-ordinary is placed below its normal position in a shield by removing a part thereof, it is termed *lowered*. *See Page* 23, *Figure* 5.

LOZENGE: A diamond shaped charge. The arms of ladies are always shown on a lozenge shaped shield. *See Page* 25, *Figure* 39, *and Page* 35, *Figure* 14.

LOZENGEE: Semee of lozenges.

LUCY: Name of a fish.

LYMPHAD: *See galley.*

MANCHE: A long flowing sleeve. *See Page* 67, *Figure* 3.

MANED: Same as *armed*, but referring to an animal's mane.

MANTLE: A long robe denoting dignity; also a figure in Heraldry. *See Page* 21, *Figure* 20.

MANTLET — MANTLING: *See lambrequin. Page* 13, *last Paragraph.*

MARSHAL: Verb — to place in proper order.

MARTLET: A chimerical bird without feet, the legs being erased; also a brissure for the fourth son. *See Page* 29, *Figure* 11.

MASCLE: A voided lozenge. *See voided. See Page* 25, *Figure* 38, *and Page* 52, *Figure* 21.

MASONED: Same as *armed*, but with reference to the mortar between the stones of a wall.

MEMBERED: Same as *armed*, but with reference to the legs of a bird.

MERMAID: A chimerical figure, one-half woman and fish from the hips down. *See Page* 56, *Figure* 40.

METAL: In Heraldry, only silver and gold are used.

MILLRIND: *See Fer de Moline.*

MITRE: An ecclesiastical headpiece. *See Page* 73, *Figure* 12.

MOLINE: *See cross moline and Fer de Moline. See Page* 21, *Figure* 5.

MOND: A sphere encircled horizontally with a band, and half encircled front to back, and ensigned by a cross, usually by a cross pattee. *See Page* 52, *Figure* 12.

MOTTO: *See Page* 10, *last Paragraph.*

MOUNT: *See compartment.*

MOUNTAIN LION: *See Page* 37, *Figure* 21.

MULLET: A spur rowel or five pointed star. If the number of points is more than five, the number must be given. It is the brissure of the third son. *See Page* 19, *cadency, also Page* 35, *Figure* 12.

MULLET PIERCED: Revel. *See Page* 42, *Figure* 9.

MURAILE: Walled.

MURAL CROWN: *See Page* 37, *Figure* 21.

MUZZLED: Wearing a muzzle, or used the same way as *armed. See Page* 37, *Figure* 8.

NAIANT: Swimming, or a fish in a horizontal position. *See Page* 54, *Figure* 2.

NAISSANT: Coming out of. Refers to figures coming out of an ordinary. *See issuant, jessant,* and *assurgant. See Page* 27, *Figure* 9.

NEBULE — NEBULY: A form of a line. *See Page* 19, *lines.*

NOMBRIL POINT: *See Page* 17, *divisions of the shield.*

NOWED: Knotted. Used to describe wivern tails, etc. *See Page* 52, *Figure* 5.

NOWY: *See franche.*

OCTOFOILE: Eight leaves cojoined in the center; a mark of cadency of the ninth son. *See Page* 19, *cadency.*

OGRESSES: *See roundels.*

ONDE — UNDY — WAVY: A form of a line. *See Page* 19, *lines.*

ORANGES: *See roundels.*

ORB: *See mond.*

ORDINARY: Honourable ordinaries are the basic shapes used in early Heraldic blazoning. They are pale, bend, chief, chevron, cross, fess, and saltire. These were then divided into dimunitives which will be found listed under each of the ordinaries. The subordinate ordinaries are billet, bordure, canton, fret, flanche, fusil, mascle, lozenge, rustre, gyron, tressure, quarter, roundel, inescutcheon, flasque, voider, and annulet. The subordinate ordinaries are shown on *Page* 25.

ORLE: An open inescutcheon, one-half the width of a bordure. Its dimunitive is the tressure. *See Page* 25, *Figure* 26.

OTTER: *See Page* 42, *Figure* 38.

OVERALL — SURTOUT: *See Page* 27, *Figure* 8.

PALE: An honourable ordinary, vertical in the center of the shield, occupying one-third thereof. *See Page* 21, *Figure* 16, *ordinaries.* This term is compounded to indicate a vertical or center vertical position; *in pale* or *paleways,* and to explain partitions *per pale, Page* 21, *Figure* 11. The pale has two dimunitives:

    PALLET: One-half the width of a *pale. See Page* 52, *Figures* 17 *and* 38.

    ENDORSE: One-fourth the width of a *pale,* and one-half the width of a *pallet.*

    PALY: Covered with a series of *pales, pallets,* or *endorses* of alternate colour and metal. *See Page* 17, *Bottom* 8.

PALL: An ecclesiastical bearing shaped like a letter Y.

PALLET: *See pale.*

PALLY — PALY: *See pale.*

PALEWAYS: *See pale.*

PANACHE: Feathers banded and erect. *See Page* 56, *Figure* 21.

PARTED — PARTY: Divided. *See Page* 21, *partitions of the field.*

PASCHAL LAMB — HOLY LAMB: *See Page* 44, *Figures* 38 *and* 40.

PASSANT: A position of a figure standing in profile, with one forepaw uplifted. *See Page* 27, *Figure* 2, *and Page* 29, *Figure* 12.

PATONCE: *See cross patonce Page* 42, *Figure* 30.

PATRIARCHAL CROSS: *See crosses Page* 19.

PEAN: A fur with gold tufts on a black field.

PEACOCK: *See Page* 56, *Figure* 8.

PEGASUS: From mythology, a winged horse. *See Page* 34, *Figure* 8, *and Page* 58, *Figure* 16.

PELLETS: Ogresses; *see roundels.*

PENCELS: Small pennons. *See Page* 32, *Figure* 8.

PENDANT: Hanging; refers to a shield suspended by a cord or chain.

PENNONCELS: Small pennons used to decorate the helmet.

PENNONS: Small flags. *See Page* 60, *Figure* 53.

PERFORATED: Pierced through the center or fess point. *See Page* 19, *Figure* 1.

PHEON: A barb, missile. *See Page* 52, *Figure* 37.

PIERCED: *See perforated.*

PIETY: Applies to a bird in its nest vulning to feed its young. *See Page* 52, *Figures* 3 *and* 29, *and Page* 54, *Figures* 4 *and* 5.

PILE: A figure whose shape is that of an isosceles triangle. The base or wide part of the triangle is usually *in chief. See Page* 25, *Figure* 27. *In pile,* arranged in the shape of a *pile. See Page* 34, *Figure* 7, *Arms of Cheney.*

PLATE: *See roundels.*

PLENTITUDE: Full; a moon in her plentitude is a full moon. *See Page* 23, *Figure* 27.

POINT IN POINT: An ordinary divided by deep serrations. *See Page* 64, *Figure* 2.

POMEIS: *See roundels.*

POMETTY: *See cross pometty Page* 19, *Figure* 10.

POMMELLED: *See cross pommelled Page* 21, *Figure* 4; also used when the pommel of a sword is of a different tincture from the hilt.

PORTCULLIS: A heavy iron grating inside a castle entrance. It could be raised by a winch to permit entry. *See Page* 30, *Figure* 5.

POTENT: *See cross potent Page* 21, *Figure* 2; also form of a line. *See Page* 19, *lines.*

POWDERED: *See semee.*

PRETENSE: *See Escutcheons of Pretense Page* 25, *Figure* 23.

PRIDE: A peacock displayed is *in its pride.*

PROPER: Figures shown in their natural colour are termed *proper.*

PUNNING — PUNNING ARMS: *See Arms Parlantes.*

PURPURE: Purple. *See Page* 17, *tinctures.*

PURSUIVANTS: Assistants to Heralds. *See Page* 8. *Paragraph* 2.

QUADRATE: Square.

QUARTER: One-fourth of a shield.

QUARTERED — QUARTERLY — PER QUARTER: Denotes that a shield is divided into four parts. *See Page* 21, *Figure* 15.

QUARTERFOILE: Four leaves conjoined in the center. *See Page* 25, *Figure* 35.

QUARTER PIERCED: Perforated with a square hole. *See Page* 19, *Figure* 6.

RADIANT — RAYONEE: Having rays. *See Page* 23, *Figure* 28.

RAGULY: Ragged. A form of a line. *See Page* 19, *lines. See cross raguly.* Also refers to tree trunks with the branches couped. *See Page* 35, *Figure* 8.

RAMPANT: A profile view of a beast standing erect on its sinister hind leg, with both forelegs elevated, the dexter above the sinister. *See Page* 27, *Figures* 4 *and* 5.

RAY: A stream of light. *See Page 19, lines.*

RAYANT — RAYONEE: *See radiant. See Page 42, Figure* 28.

REBATED: Diminished. *See Page 23, Figure 10.*

REFLEXED: Curved backwards. *See Page 65, Figure 4.*

REVEL — ROWELL: A mullet pierced. *See Page 42, Figure 9.*

REGUARDANT: A position of the head; turned backwards. *See Page 27, Figure 4.*

REST: A rest or socket for the butt of a lance. *See clarion.*

RIBAND: *See bend.*

RISING: A position of a bird about to take flight. *See Page 29, Figure 9, and Page 34, Figure 5.*

ROUNDELS: A roundel is a disk; in Heraldry it is shown as a circle. Roundels have specific names for each tincture or treatment. Below is an alphabetical list of these terms:

> BESANTS — BEZANTS — BYZANTS: Gold roundels. *See Page 25, Figure 6.*
>
> FOUNTAINS: Roundels barry wavy of six — silver and blue.
>
> GOLPS: Purple roundels.
>
> GUZES: Sanguine (dark red) roundels.
>
> HURTS: Blue roundels.
>
> OGRESSES — PELLETS: Black roundels.
>
> ORANGES: Tenne or tawny roundels.
>
> PLATES: Silver roundels.
>
> POMEIS: Green roundels.
>
> TORTEAUX: Red roundels.

A double E added to any of the above terms denotes that the object charged is *semee* of that particular roundel; for example, *besantee* means *semee*, or strewed, with gold roundels.

ROSTRE — RUSTRE: A lozenge having a round opening. *See Page 25, Figure 37.*

SABLE: Black. *See Page 17 tinctures.*

SALIENT: A position similar to *rampant*, except that both hind paws are on the ground, and the body is not as erect, but more in a leaping position. *See counter salient. See Page 25, Figure 45, and Page 42, Figure 14.*

SALTIRE: An honourable ordinary; a cross formed by a bend crossing a bend sinister. Like a bend, the saltire occupies one-fifth of the shield if uncharged; if charged, it occupies one-third of the shield. It is also known as the Cross of St. Andrew of Scotland, and St. Patrick of Ireland. *See Page 17, Bottom 7. In saltire* denotes arrangement of figures in the form of an X. *See Page 31, Figures 11 and 14.*

SANGLIER: A boar.

SANGUINE — MURREY: *See Page 17, tinctures.*

SCEPTER — SCEPTRE: A staff of command or sovereignty. *See Page 60, Figure 31.*

SCIMITAR: A curved sword. *See Page 60, Figure 18.*

SCRAPE: *See bend.*

SCROLL: A band upon which the motto is inscribed. *See Page 10.*

SEA HORSE: In Heraldry, a mythical figure — half horse and half fish. *See Page 58, Figures 29 and 31.*

SEEDED: The same as *armed,* but referring to seeds of a flower.

SEGREANT: A position of the wings of a dragon, griffin, or wivern. *See Page 29, Figure 7, and Page 37, Figure 17.*

SEJANT: *See assise. See Page 27, Figure 10, and Page 34, Figure 4.*

SEJANT ERECT: Sitting position of a squirrel. *See Page 58, Figures 44, 45, and 46.*

SEMEE: Strewed, sprinkled, powdered. *See Page 25, Figure 4.*

SETFOILE: Six leaves conjoined at the center.

SHAKEFORK: A charge whose shape is that of the letter Y.

SIGNET LETTER: A roll of parchment. *See Page 52, Figures 17 and 38.*

SINISTER: Left. *See Page 35, Figure 19, and Page 14, Paragraph 2.*

SLIPPED: The stem torn from the branch, or leaves torn from the stem. *See Page 35, Figure 18.*

SOL: The sun in its splendour, or glory; represented by a circle *figured* and *rayant. See figured. See rayant. See Page 37, Figure 14.*

SOVEREIGN: A ruler or king.

SOVEREIGN CROWN: Crown of a Sovereign. *See Page 60, Figure 37.*

SPLENDOUR: *See sol.*

SPROUTING AFRESH: *See accrued.*

SQUARE PIERCED: *See quarter pierced.*

STAFF: *See crosier.* Also a staff of big wheat. *See Page 38, Figure 3.*

STAR: *See estoile and mullet.*

STATANT: Standing. *See Page 34, Figure 1, and Page 42, Figure 17.*

STEPWAYS: *See embattled grady.*

SUPPORTERS: *See Page 15, Paragraph 3.*

SURCOAT: *See coat armour.*

SURMOUNTED: Placed over, overlying. *See Page 25, Figure 2, and Page 34, Figure 5.*

SURTOUT: Overall. A term used when one ordinary is placed over another ordinary. *See Page 27, Figure 8, describing arms.*

TABARD: A tunic worn by Heralds and pursuivants. *See Page 8.*

TALBOT: A hunting dog. *See Page 42, Figures 10, 28, and 34.*

TAWNY — TENNE: Orange tincture. *See Page 17, tinctures.*

THISTLE: A vigorous plant — the Emblem of Scotland. *See Page 40, Figure 41.*

TIERCED: Divided into three portions.

TINCTURE: Colour, metal, or fur. *See engravers' trick and Page 17, tinctures.*

TORSE: *See Page 13, Paragraph 2.*

TORTEAUX: *See roundels.*

TORTILLY: Wreathed.

TRANSPOSED: Placed in the reverse of the normal position.

TRAVERSE: *See Page 21, Figure 22.*

TREFOILE: Three leaves and a stem *wavy;* the shamrock of Ireland. *See Page 25, Figure 34, and Page 32, Figure 6.*

TRESSURE: *See bordure.*

TRICORPORATED: Three animals cojoined, having a common head.

TRICK: *See engravers' trick.*

TRIDENT: A three tined spear. *See Page 58, Figure 34.*

TRIPPANT: Tripping; the gait of a deer between running and walking. *See Page 27, Figure 28, and Page 46, Figure 21.*

TRUSSED: *See close.*

TUSKED: Same as *armed,* but referring to tusks.

TYNED: *See attired. See Page 27, Figure 31.*

TYNES: Antlers.

UNDE — UNDY: *See onde.*

UNICORN: A mythical animal; a horse with a single horn. *See Page 58, Figures 4 and 6.*

UNVESTED: Not vested, naked. *See Page 34, Figure 12.*

URCHIN: Hedgehog.

URDE: A form of a line, similar to a *vair. See Page 21, Figure 13.*

VAIR: Classed as a fur, blue bells on a silver field unless otherwise specified. *See Page 17, tinctures.*

VAMBRACED: Armoured; applies only to armour for humans. *See Page 34, Figure 13.*

90

VAMPLATE: The armour on a lance designed to protect the hand.

VERDEE — VERDOY: A *semee* of flowers, leaves, etc.

VERT: Green. *See Page* 17, *tinctures.*

VESTED: Dressed, clothed. *See Page* 35, *Figure* 5.

VESTU: *See Page* 23, *Figure* 29.

VISOR: The grating or vertical bars in the front of a helmet to protect the eyes. *See Page* 13, *Paragraph* 3.

VOIDED: When a part of an ordinary is left open to the field, the ordinary is termed *voided.* What it actually amounts to is that the ordinary is outlined. *See Page* 19, *Figure* 2.

VOIDER: *See Page* 25, *Figure* 28.

VOLANT: Flying. *See Page* 56, *Figure* 23.

VORANT: Eating, devouring. *See Page* 58, *Figure* 41.

VULNED: Wounded.

VULNING: Wounding itself. *See piety.*

WALLED: *See embattled.*

WATERED: Made up of wavy lines to resemble water. *See Page* 19, *Figure* 7.

WATTLED: Having a comb; also used the same as *armed.*

WAVY: *See undy.*

WINDOWED: Same as *armed,* referring to the tincture of windows.

WINGED: Having wings; also used same as *armed.*

WINGS DISCLOSED: Open and pointed downward. *See Page* 52, *Figure* 8, *and Page* 31, *Figure* 15.

WINGS DISPLAYED: Open and pointed up. *See Page* 34, *Figure* 8.

WINGS ERECT: Pointed up. *See Page* 37, *Figure* 11.

WINGS INVERTED: Pointed downward. *See Page* 34, *Figure* 8.

WINGS IN PRIDE: *See pride.*

WINGS SEGREANT: In profile and pointed upward. *See Page* 37, *Figure* 17.

WIVERN: A chimerical beast, half dragon with its tail nowed. *See Page* 48.

WOLF: A canine animal. *See Page* 48, *Figure* 4.

WOLVERINE: Canine animal. *See Page* 31, *Figure* 12.

WREATH: *See Page* 13, *Paragraph* 2.

Paradigm of the Tinctures.

Names.	Colours.	Stones.	Planets.	Planets.	Metals.	Latin Names.	Abbreviations.	Signs of the Zodiac.	Months.	Days of the Week.	Elements.	Seasons and times of Day.	Ages.	Tempers.	Virtues.	Flowers.	Numbers.
Or	Yellow	Topaz	Sol	☉	Gold	Aureus	O	Leo	July	Sunday	Light	Noon	Adolescence	Blithe	Force	Heliotrope	1, 3
Argent	White	Pearl	Luna	☽	Silver	Argenteus	Ar.	Cancer	June	Monday	Water	Morning	Infancy	Phlegmatic	Hope	Lily	2, 12
Gules	Red	Ruby	Mars	♂	Iron	Ruber	G	Aries and Scorpio	March and Octob.	Tuesday	Fire	Autumn	Manhood	Choleric	Charity	Rose	10
Azure	Blue	Sapphire	Jupiter	♃	Tin	Cæruleus	Az.b	Taurus and Libra	April and Sept.	Thursday	Air	Summer	Childhood	Sanguine	Justice	Blue Bell	4, 9
Vert	Green	Emerald	Venus	♀	Copper	Viridis	Vt.	Gemini and Virgo	May & August	Friday	Life	Spring	Youth	Bilious	Strength	The field	6, 11
Purpure	Purple	Amethyst	Mercury	☿	Quick-Silver	Purpureus	Pur.	Sagittarius and Pisces	Nov. & Feb.	Wednes.	Thunderbolt	Evening	Old Age	Serious	Temperance	Iris	7
Sable	Black	Diamond	Saturn	♄	Lead	Niger	S	Capricorn and Amphora	Dec. & Jan.	Saturday	Earth	Winter and Night	Decrepitude	Melancholy	Prudence	Scabiosa	5, 8

Heraldry was studied and followed with great enthusiasm during the dark ages of superstition. It was applied to the Caballistic secrets of numbers, the complexion, age, and temper of a man; the elements of nature, the Constellations, the Zodiac, metals of the Earth, stones, etc.

We have here reproduced a paradigm taken from the *Encyclopaedia Londinensis* which gives a concise synopsis of this fanciful system.

92